Echoes of Storrington

Timeless Echoes

Angeline Gallant

Published by Crest & Quill Press, 2024.

While every precaution has been taken in the preparation of this book, the publisher assumes no responsibility for errors or omissions, or for damages resulting from the use of the information contained herein.

ECHOES OF STORRINGTON

First edition. December 4, 2024.

Copyright © 2024 Angeline Gallant.

ISBN: 979-8230197317

Written by Angeline Gallant.

Table of Contents

JANE SMITH 1

JAMES SMITH 10

ELIZEBETH SMITH 16

MARY A. SMITH 22

JANE SMITH 27

CHARLES SMITH 31

MARY (UNKNOWN) JOHNSTON 35

CHARLES SMITH 43

CAROLINE (UNKNOWN) SMITH 49

ELIZEBETH SMITH 54

SIMEON SMITH 58

MARGARET SMITH 62

CORNEUS SMITH 66

JAMES SMITH 72

ROSEY SHAW 78

WILLIAM STEWART 83

MARTHA (UNKNOWN) STEWART 90

PEETER STEWART 96

REBECCA STEWART 101

ALEX McWATTERS	106
MARGARET (UNKNOWN) McWATTERS	112
MARGARET McWATTERS	120
CATHRINE McWATTERS	124
JOHN McWATTERS	128
CATHRINE McWATTERS	140
THOMAS McWATTERS	151
MARY (UNKNOWN) McWATTERS	155
JOHN ISRAEL JOHNSTON	158
SARAH MIRIAM (GORDON) JOHNSTON	165
JAMES JOHNSTON	176
WILLIAM JOHNSTON	183
MARY SEREPTA JOHNSTON	188
ANNE JOHNSTON	190
JANE JOHNSTON	193
ELIZABETH JOHNSTON	198
JOHN LINDSAY	201
MARGERET (BALLENTYNE) LINDSAY	208
SAMUEL LINDSAY	211
MARTHA LINDSAY	214
THOMAS LINDSAY	219

ELIZABETH ANN LINDSAY 225

JOSEPH ALLEN LINDSAY 230

MARY JANE LINDSAY 232

THOMAS YOUNG 234

MARTHA (UNKNOWN) YOUNG 241

JOHN YOUNG 246

WILLIAM YOUNG 249

RICHARD YOUNG 251

FRANCIS BLESSON 252

JANE SMITH

JANE SMITH[1]

In 1833, Ireland was a predominantly rural and agrarian society, with most people relying on small-scale farming or tenant farming for their livelihood. The population was rapidly growing, nearing 8 million, which would contribute to increased land pressure and poverty in the coming years.

Life for the rural poor:

The majority of Irish families lived in simple one-room cottages, often with thatched roofs. Subsistence farming was common, with the potato as the primary food source due to its high yield and nutritional value. However, dependency on this single crop made families vulnerable to disease and famine, a foreshadowing of the Great Famine just over a decade later.

Social structure and tenant farming:

Ireland was deeply divided by class. Wealthy landlords, often of Anglo-Irish descent, owned most of the land, which was leased to tenant farmers. These tenants were required to pay rent, frequently leaving them with little to support their families. Evictions were common for those unable to pay, leading to widespread instability.

Religion and politics:

Ireland in 1833 was shaped by the recent passage of the Catholic Emancipation Act (1829), which allowed Catholics to hold political office and reduced some long standing restrictions. Despite this, tensions between Catholics and Protestants remained high, and many

Catholics continued to face discrimination. Politically, Daniel O'Connell, known as "The Liberator," was leading efforts for Irish self-governance (Repeal of the Union) and greater rights for Catholics.

Urban life and emigration:

Cities like Dublin, Cork, and Belfast were growing, but urban life was challenging for the poor, with overcrowding and unsanitary conditions. Industrialization was slower in Ireland compared to England, although Belfast was emerging as a hub for linen production. Some families began emigrating to North America or Australia in search of better opportunities, though this trend would accelerate significantly after the famine.

For a woman like Jane Smith, born into this setting, her life would largely depend on her family's socioeconomic status. If her family were farmers, she might have spent her early years helping with household and agricultural duties. Education was limited, especially for girls, although the establishment of National Schools in 1831 meant she might have had access to basic education if her family could afford the time and cost.

WHEN JANE SMITH WAS six years old, the Irish Hurricane of 1839, also known as the Night of the Big Wind ("Oíche na Gaoithe Móire"), swept across Ireland on the night of January 6–7, 1839. This was one of the most catastrophic storms in Irish history and left a lasting impact on the people and the land.

What happened during the storm?

The hurricane brought ferocious winds that destroyed homes, churches, and barns across Ireland.

Entire forests were uprooted, and fires broke out as winds fanned the flames of household hearths.

It caused widespread flooding as rivers overflowed their banks.

Thousands of people were left homeless, and many sought refuge in churches or with neighbors.

IMPACT ON FAMILIES like Jane's:

If Jane's family was still in Ireland at the time, they would have experienced the storm firsthand. The hurricane struck both rural and urban areas, devastating crops and causing massive property damage. Families already struggling due to poverty faced even greater hardship in the aftermath, with limited resources to rebuild.

Cultural Memory:

The Night of the Big Wind became a defining moment in Irish history and folklore. It was so significant that survivors would reference it for decades, and it was even used as a benchmark when assessing old-age pension eligibility in later years ("Were you alive during the Big Wind?").

For Jane, this event might have been one of the earliest major historical memories of her childhood, especially if her family was directly affected. It could have also influenced their decision to emigrate, as the storm highlighted the vulnerability of life in Ireland during a time of economic and social challenges.

AT THE AGE OF 12, JANE Smith would have witnessed or been affected by the mass Irish immigration sparked by the Great Famine

(1845–1852) if her family had not already emigrated. The year 1845 marked the beginning of the potato blight, which devastated the primary food source for much of Ireland's population, leading to starvation, disease, and widespread emigration.

Life in 1845 and the Irish Immigration:

The Potato Blight: A fungal disease (Phytophthora infestans) infected potato crops, causing them to rot and become inedible. Potatoes were a dietary staple for the majority of Irish people, particularly rural communities.

Economic and Social Collapse: As the blight spread, tenant farmers were unable to pay rent, leading to mass evictions and destitution. Hunger and poverty increased rapidly.

Mass Emigration: To escape starvation, many Irish families emigrated to countries like Canada, the United States, and Australia. Ships carrying immigrants were often overcrowded and disease-ridden, earning the grim nickname "coffin ships."

IMPACT ON JANE AND Her Family:

If Jane and her family were still in Ireland at the time, they would have faced severe economic and social pressures. The upheaval of 1845 likely shaped their worldview, as entire communities were uprooted. If they had already emigrated to Canada, they would have encountered a surge of Irish immigrants arriving in desperate conditions. This influx shaped the communities in places like Storrington, Ontario, where Jane later lived.

Broader Significance:

The Irish immigration of 1845 and beyond became one of the largest movements of people in the 19th century. For Jane, this would have been a defining historical moment of her youth, as her Irish heritage connected her to the struggles of those fleeing famine and seeking new opportunities abroad.

BY 1861, JANE SMITH, now living in Storrington Township, Ontario, would have been part of a growing and changing community in Canada West (modern-day Ontario). Storrington, located near Kingston, was a rural area where agriculture was the dominant way of life.

Religious and Social Life:

As a Presbyterian, Jane was part of a religious community that emphasized education, moral discipline, and community worship. Presbyterianism was one of the prominent Protestant denominations in Canada at the time, especially among Scottish and Irish immigrants. Churches often served as not only spiritual centers but also places for social gatherings and mutual support.

Life in Storrington Township:

Storrington in the mid-19th century was characterized by small farms, forests, and rural settlements. Families were largely self-sufficient, growing their own food and raising livestock. Lumbering was also an important industry in the area, contributing to the local economy. Daily life involved hard work, particularly for women, who managed household chores, cared for children, and assisted with farming tasks.

Canada in 1861:

This was a time of rapid growth and change in Canada. The population of Canada West was expanding due to immigration, particularly from Ireland, Scotland, and England. The year 1861 marked a federal census, capturing detailed snapshots of the lives of Canadians. Railways were beginning to connect rural areas to larger towns and cities, facilitating trade and travel. Political discussions about Confederation (which would occur in 1867) were intensifying, as leaders debated the future of Canada as a united country.

Cultural and Family Life:

Jane's daily life would have revolved around her family, neighbors, and church. Social gatherings often took place around religious holidays, weddings, or community events. If she had children, education would likely have been important, with rural schools providing basic literacy and numeracy skills. Access to goods and news from Kingston or other larger towns would have been possible but limited to what could be transported by wagon or boat.

For a woman of Jane's background, the transition from her Irish roots to Canadian rural life would have been marked by hard work, faith, and the slow but steady integration into the fabric of a developing nation.

GENEALOGY TRAVEL ITINERARY:

Day 1: Arrival in Dublin, Ireland

• Morning: Arrive in Dublin and check into your hotel.

• Afternoon: Visit the National Archives of Ireland to explore records from the 1830s.

• Evening: Enjoy a traditional Irish dinner at a local pub.

Day 2: Dublin Historical Sites

- Morning: Tour Dublin Castle, which has a rich history dating back to the 13th century

Ireland's Most Scenic Historic Sites | Historical Landmarks | History Hit[1]

- AFTERNOON: VISIT Mount Melleray Abbey, founded in 1833, to get a sense of the religious landscape during Jane's birth year

1833 in Ireland - Wikipedia[2]

- EVENING: STROLL ALONG the River Liffey and enjoy the vibrant city life.

Day 3: Journey to County Cork

- Morning: Travel to County Cork, where many Irish emigrants originated.

- Afternoon: Visit Blarney Castle and kiss the famous Blarney Stone

Ireland's Most Scenic Historic Sites | Historical Landmarks | History Hit[3]

- EVENING: EXPLORE the local countryside and stay overnight in a charming bed and breakfast.

Day 4: Exploring Ancestral Roots

---

1. https://www.historyhit.com/guides/historic-sites-in-ireland/

2. https://en.wikipedia.org/wiki/1833_in_Ireland

3. https://www.historyhit.com/guides/historic-sites-in-ireland/

- Morning: Visit local churches and cemeteries to search for any records or gravesites that might be connected to Jane's family.

- Afternoon: Meet with a local genealogist to discuss findings and gather more information.

- Evening: Return to Dublin and prepare for your flight to Canada.

Day 5: Arrival in Kingston, Ontario

- Morning: Arrive in Kingston, Ontario, and check into your hotel.

- Afternoon: Visit the Frontenac County Schools Museum to understand the local history of the area where Jane lived.

- Evening: Enjoy a relaxing evening by the waterfront.

Day 6: Storrington, Ontario

- Morning: Travel to Storrington and visit the Storrington Presbyterian Church, where Jane might have worshipped.

- Afternoon: Explore local archives and historical societies for records from the 1860s.

- Evening: Visit local landmarks and enjoy the serene countryside.

Day 7: Reflect and Explore

- Morning: Visit local cemeteries to find Jane's gravesite or any family markers.

- Afternoon: Take a scenic drive around the area, visiting any other historical sites or landmarks.

- Evening: Return to Kingston for a farewell dinner.

Day 8: Departure

- Morning: Reflect on your journey and gather any final records or souvenirs.

- Afternoon: Depart from Kingston, Ontario.

This itinerary combines historical research with cultural experiences, making it a meaningful trip to honour Jane Smith's legacy. Safe travels!

JAMES SMITH

JAMES SMITH[2]

James Smith was born in 1853 in Upper Canada (modern-day Ontario), during a period of significant change and growth in the colony. His birth took place in a society still shaped by its British colonial roots but increasingly developing its own identity.

Life in Upper Canada in 1853:

Political Context: The Act of Union (1841) had merged Upper and Lower Canada into the Province of Canada, with Upper Canada becoming Canada West. Discussions about responsible government and confederation were becoming more prominent.

Economic Growth: The mid-19th century saw improvements in infrastructure, including railways, canals, and roads. Kingston, where many families settled, had been an important military and economic hub, though Toronto and Montreal were growing as commercial centers.

Agriculture and Settlements: Rural life dominated Canada West. Farming was the primary occupation, and families like the Smiths likely relied on agriculture or trade for their livelihood.

Social Conditions: Immigration was reshaping the population, with Irish, Scottish, and other settlers arriving in large numbers. Social hierarchies were influenced by land ownership, religion, and British ties.

EVENTS OF 1853:

Railway Expansion: The construction of the Grand Trunk Railway, connecting communities across Canada West, began around this time, spurring economic growth and making travel easier.

Education Reform: Efforts to establish public schools under the Common Schools Act were underway, which would have shaped James's education during his youth.

Cultural Influence: British traditions heavily influenced daily life, including religion, language, and governance, though a distinct Canadian identity was emerging.

AS A BOY BORN IN THIS era, James Smith grew up in a period of transition, laying the groundwork for the future of Ontario and Canada as a nation.

IN 1861, JAMES SMITH, at 8 years old, was living in Storrington, Ontario, with his family and identified as Presbyterian, reflecting the strong Scottish heritage prevalent in the area.

Life in Storrington, Ontario, in 1861:

Rural Community: Storrington was a small township in Frontenac County, characterized by farming and rural life. Most families, including the Smiths, likely lived on farms or worked in trades supporting the agricultural economy.

Religion: Presbyterianism was a dominant faith among Scottish immigrants and their descendants, influencing local culture, community gatherings, and education. Churches often served as central meeting places for both worship and social interaction.

Education: By 1861, Ontario had implemented a public school system under the Common Schools Act. James may have attended a one-room schoolhouse, learning basic literacy, arithmetic, and religious teachings rooted in Presbyterian values.

Census of 1861: This was the first detailed census conducted in Canada, reflecting demographic and economic information. James's family would have been recorded, listing their religious affiliation, occupation, and household details.

HISTORICAL CONTEXT:

Confederation Movement: Although Confederation was still six years away, discussions about uniting the provinces were gaining momentum.

Population Growth: Immigration, particularly from Ireland and Scotland, continued to shape Ontario, contributing to a diverse yet predominantly British colonial culture.

Daily Life: Life revolved around the rhythms of farm work and church activities. Children like James likely helped with chores and experienced a disciplined upbringing influenced by religious teachings.

JAMES'S CHILDHOOD IN Storrington provided him with a foundation deeply rooted in faith, hard work, and the traditions of a developing rural community in pre-Confederation Canada.

GENEALOGY ITINERARY:

Day 1: Arrival in Kingston, Ontario

• Morning: Arrive in Kingston and check into your hotel.

• Afternoon: Visit the Kingston Navy Yard National Historic Site to get a sense of the area's history during the mid-19th century

https://www.historicplaces.ca/en/rep-reg/place-lieu.aspx?id=10484

———————

• EVENING: ENJOY A relaxing dinner by the waterfront.

Day 2: Kingston Historical Sites

• Morning: Tour the Frontenac County Schools Museum to understand the local education system during James's childhood.

• Afternoon: Visit Bellevue House, the former home of Sir John A. Macdonald, to learn about life in Upper Canada during the 1850s

https://www.historicplaces.ca/en/rep-reg/place-lieu.aspx?id=10484

———————

• EVENING: EXPLORE downtown Kingston and its historic architecture.

Day 3: Journey to Storrington, Ontario

• Morning: Travel to Storrington and visit the Storrington Presbyterian Church, where James might have worshipped.

• Afternoon: Explore local archives and historical societies for records from the 1860s.

• Evening: Stay overnight in a local bed and breakfast.

Day 4: Exploring Ancestral Roots

- Morning: Visit local cemeteries to search for James's gravesite or any family markers.

- Afternoon: Meet with a local genealogist to discuss findings and gather more information.

- Evening: Return to Kingston and prepare for the next day's activities.

Day 5: Historical Sites in Upper Canada

- Morning: Visit Upper Canada Village, a living history museum that recreates life in the 1860s

Upper Canada Village - Wikipedia[1]

- AFTERNOON: EXPLORE the village and participate in hands-on activities to experience daily life as James might have known it.

- Evening: Return to Kingston for a relaxing evening.

Day 6: Reflect and Explore

- Morning: Take a scenic drive around the area, visiting any other historical sites or landmarks.

- Afternoon: Visit the Royal Military College of Canada to learn about its history and significance during James's time

https://www.historicplaces.ca/en/rep-reg/place-lieu.aspx?id=10484

- EVENING: ENJOY A farewell dinner in Kingston.

---

1. https://en.wikipedia.org/wiki/Upper_Canada_Village

Day 7: Departure

- Morning: Reflect on your journey and gather any final records or souvenirs.

- Afternoon: Depart from Kingston, Ontario.

This itinerary combines historical research with cultural experiences, making it a meaningful trip to honor James Smith's legacy.

ELIZEBETH SMITH

ELIZEBETH SMITH[3]

Elizabeth Smith was born in 1854 in Upper Canada, a time when the region was undergoing significant growth and change. Upper Canada (now Ontario) was developing rapidly due to immigration, agricultural expansion, and improvements in infrastructure.

Life in Upper Canada in 1854:

Agricultural Economy: Farming was the backbone of life, with families relying on crops like wheat, oats, and barley. Elizabeth was likely born into a rural environment where farm life shaped daily routines.

Religion: As part of a Presbyterian family, religious life would have played a central role. Church attendance, Sunday school, and adherence to moral values were important aspects of upbringing.

Transportation: 1854 marked the opening of major railways, such as the Grand Trunk Railway, which connected communities and improved access to markets and goods. This transformation started influencing rural communities like those in Upper Canada.

HISTORICAL EVENTS:

Reciprocity Treaty: In 1854, the Reciprocity Treaty was signed between Canada and the U.S., boosting trade and helping farmers export goods like grain and timber.

Crimean War: Internationally, the Crimean War (1853–1856) affected global trade, including Canadian exports, and influenced colonial perspectives on the British Empire.

ELIZABETH'S EARLY YEARS were shaped by a society that balanced traditional rural values with the beginnings of industrial and economic modernization, laying the groundwork for Canada's eventual Confederation.

IN 1861, ELIZABETH Smith was 7 years old, living in Storrington, Ontario, and part of a Presbyterian household. Life in rural Ontario at that time revolved around family, farming, and community life.

Storrington, Ontario in 1861:

Rural Community: Storrington was a township in Frontenac County, characterized by its agricultural economy. Families like Elizabeth's likely lived on farms, growing crops and raising livestock to sustain themselves.

Presbyterian Faith: Religion would have been a cornerstone of her upbringing. Presbyterian families emphasized education, morality, and regular church attendance. Sunday worship was a key part of the week, and children were taught catechism and Bible lessons.

LIFE FOR A 7-YEAR-OLD:

Education: By 1861, basic schooling was becoming more accessible. Elizabeth might have attended a one-room schoolhouse where she learned reading, writing, arithmetic, and religious instruction.

Household Chores: Even at a young age, children contributed to the family. Elizabeth might have helped with small tasks like fetching water, tending to chickens, or helping her mother with household chores.

Community: Neighbors often worked together during harvests or barn-raising events, fostering a strong sense of community in rural areas like Storrington.

BROADER CONTEXT IN 1861:

Census of 1861: This was the year of Canada's first comprehensive census, recording demographic and economic details about families like Elizabeth's.

Pre-Confederation Canada: Ontario was still part of the Province of Canada. Discussions about Confederation were starting to take shape, but rural families focused on their daily lives rather than politics.

ELIZABETH'S EARLY LIFE would have been marked by simplicity, hard work, and close-knit family ties in a growing and changing Upper Canada.

GENEALOGY ITINERARY:

Day 1: Arrival in Kingston, Ontario

• Morning: Arrive in Kingston and check into your hotel.

• Afternoon: Visit the Kingston Penitentiary Museum to learn about the history of the area during the mid-19th century

Stayner (formerly Nottawasaga Station)[1]

- EVENING: ENJOY A relaxing dinner by the waterfront.

Day 2: Kingston Historical Sites

- Morning: Tour the Frontenac County Schools Museum to understand the local education system during Elizabeth's childhood.

- Afternoon: Visit Bellevue House, the former home of Sir John A. Macdonald, to learn about life in Upper Canada during the 1850s

Stayner (formerly Nottawasaga Station)[2]

- EVENING: EXPLORE downtown Kingston and its historic architecture.

Day 3: Journey to Storrington, Ontario

- Morning: Travel to Storrington and visit the Storrington Presbyterian Church, where Elizabeth might have worshipped

https://www.archeion.ca/st-andrews-presbyterian-church-sunbury-ont

- AFTERNOON: EXPLORE local archives and historical societies for records from the 1860s.

- Evening: Stay overnight in a local bed and breakfast.

Day 4: Exploring Ancestral Roots

---

1. https://www.hmdb.org/m.asp?m=261793

2. https://www.hmdb.org/m.asp?m=261793

- Morning: Visit local cemeteries to search for Elizabeth's gravesite or any family markers.

- Afternoon: Meet with a local genealogist to discuss findings and gather more information.

- Evening: Return to Kingston and prepare for the next day's activities.

Day 5: Historical Sites in Upper Canada

- Morning: Visit Upper Canada Village, a living history museum that recreates life in the 1860s

Places - Settlements - Upper Canada Village[3]

- AFTERNOON: EXPLORE the village and participate in hands-on activities to experience daily life as Elizabeth might have known it.

- Evening: Return to Kingston for a relaxing evening.

Day 6: Reflect and Explore

- Morning: Take a scenic drive around the area, visiting any other historical sites or landmarks.

- Afternoon: Visit the Royal Military College of Canada to learn about its history and significance during Elizabeth's time

Stayner (formerly Nottawasaga Station)[4].

- EVENING: ENJOY A farewell dinner in Kingston.

---

3. http://www.canadahistory.com/sections/places/Settlements/Upper_Canada_Village.html

4. https://www.hmdb.org/m.asp?m=261793

Day 7: Departure

- Morning: Reflect on your journey and gather any final records or souvenirs.

- Afternoon: Depart from Kingston, Ontario.

This itinerary combines historical research with cultural experiences, making it a meaningful trip to honour Elizabeth Smith's legacy.

MARY A. SMITH

MARY A. SMITH[4]

Mary A. Smith was born in 1856 in Upper Canada (now Ontario), during a period of rapid growth and change in the province. Settlements were expanding, and the agricultural economy dominated rural life.

What Life Was Like in 1856:

Upper Canada Society: The region was transitioning toward becoming Canada West, part of the Province of Canada. This was a pre-Confederation era, marked by British influence and developing Canadian identity.

Agriculture: Most families lived on farms, growing crops like wheat and raising livestock. Self-sufficiency was crucial, and rural communities were tightly knit.

Women's Roles: Mary's mother likely managed the household, prepared food, and helped with farm duties, roles Mary would eventually learn as she grew older.

EVENTS OF 1856:

Railway Expansion: Railroads were being built across the province, connecting towns and encouraging trade and settlement.

Immigration: Many immigrants continued to arrive from Ireland, Scotland, and England, further populating Upper Canada and influencing its cultural landscape.

MARY A. SMITH'S EARLY years would have been shaped by the rhythms of rural life, family, and faith, as well as the gradual transformation of Upper Canada into a more developed society.

IN 1861, MARY A. SMITH was 5 years old, living in Storrington Township, Ontario, with her family. She was recorded as Presbyterian, reflecting the strong presence of Scottish and Irish Presbyterian immigrants in the area.

Life in Storrington, Ontario, in 1861:

Community Life: Storrington was a rural township where neighbors often worked together on tasks such as farming and building infrastructure. Churches and schools were central to community life, with Presbyterianism being a prominent faith.

Daily Routine: As a child, Mary likely helped with small household tasks or cared for younger siblings, learning the skills she would need later in life.

1861 EVENTS AND CONTEXT:

Population Growth: The township was steadily growing, with settlers clearing land and building homes, barns, and roads.

Canada's Development: The Province of Canada (modern Ontario and Quebec) was preparing for Confederation, with political discussions about uniting the British North American colonies.

MARY'S EARLY YEARS were rooted in a tight-knit, faith-driven rural community, where family, church, and local events shaped her formative experiences.

GENEALOGY ITINERARY

Day 1: Arrival in Kingston, Ontario

- Morning: Arrive in Kingston and check into your hotel.

- Afternoon: Visit the Kingston Penitentiary Museum to learn about the history of the area during the mid-19th century

The heritage of faith – Ontario's places of worship[1]

- EVENING: ENJOY A relaxing dinner by the waterfront.

Day 2: Kingston Historical Sites

- Morning: Tour the Frontenac County Schools Museum to understand the local education system during Mary's childhood.

- Afternoon: Visit Bellevue House, the former home of Sir John A. Macdonald, to learn about life in Canada West during the 1850s

The heritage of faith – Ontario's places of worship[2]

---

1. https://www.heritage-matters.ca/articles/the-heritage-of-faith-ontarios-places-of-worship
2. https://www.heritage-matters.ca/articles/the-heritage-of-faith-ontarios-places-of-worship

- EVENING: EXPLORE downtown Kingston and its historic architecture.

Day 3: Journey to Storrington, Ontario

- Morning: Travel to Storrington and visit the Storrington Presbyterian Church, where Mary might have worshipped

1856 in Canada - Wikipedia[3]

- AFTERNOON: EXPLORE local archives and historical societies for records from the 1860s.

- Evening: Stay overnight in a local bed and breakfast.

Day 4: Exploring Ancestral Roots

- Morning: Visit local cemeteries to search for Mary's gravesite or any family markers.

- Afternoon: Meet with a local genealogist to discuss findings and gather more information.

- Evening: Return to Kingston and prepare for the next day's activities.

Day 5: Historical Sites in Canada West

- Morning: Visit Upper Canada Village, a living history museum that recreates life in the 1860s.

- Afternoon: Explore the village and participate in hands-on activities to experience daily life as Mary might have known it.

- Evening: Return to Kingston for a relaxing evening.

---

3. https://en.wikipedia.org/wiki/1856_in_Canada

Day 6: Reflect and Explore

- Morning: Take a scenic drive around the area, visiting any other historical sites or landmarks.

- Afternoon: Visit the Royal Military College of Canada to learn about its history and significance during Mary's time

The heritage of faith – Ontario's places of worship[4]

- EVENING: ENJOY A farewell dinner in Kingston.

Day 7: Departure

- Morning: Reflect on your journey and gather any final records or souvenirs.

- Afternoon: Depart from Kingston, Ontario.

This itinerary combines historical research with cultural experiences, making it a meaningful trip to honour Mary A. Smith's legacy.

---

4. https://www.heritage-matters.ca/articles/the-heritage-of-faith-ontarios-places-of-worship

JANE SMITH

JANE SMITH[5]

Jane Smith was born in 1858 in Upper Canada (modern-day Ontario), during a time of significant growth and change in the region.

Context of Life in 1858:

Upper Canada: By 1858, the region was known as Canada West following the 1841 union of Upper and Lower Canada into the Province of Canada. The area was experiencing population growth due to immigration and expanding infrastructure.

Economy: Agriculture was the primary livelihood, supplemented by local trades and industries such as lumber and milling.

Daily Life: Jane's early years would have been marked by rural routines, strong family bonds, and a community-oriented way of life.

HER BIRTH IN 1858 PLACED her within a generation that would witness the Confederation of Canada in 1867 and the rapid industrial and societal changes that followed.

IN 1861, JANE SMITH was 3 years old, living with her family in Storrington, Ontario, and identified as Presbyterian.

Life in Storrington in 1861:

Rural Setting: Storrington was a small, rural township where farming and local trades dominated daily life. Families often relied on one another for support, forming close-knit communities.

Religious Influence: Presbyterianism was a significant part of life, shaping moral values, education, and community events. Churches often served as central gathering places.

Childhood Life: At 3, Jane would have been immersed in a household-oriented life, likely surrounded by siblings and extended family members, contributing to household chores as she grew.

HER LIFE IN STORRINGTON reflected the simplicity and interconnectedness of rural Ontario during the mid-19th century.

GENEALOGY ITINERARY

Day 1: Arrival in Kingston, Ontario

• Morning: Arrive in Kingston and check into your hotel.

• Afternoon: Visit the Kingston Penitentiary Museum to learn about the history of the area during the mid-19th century

Canada West | The Canadian Encyclopedia[1]

• EVENING: ENJOY A relaxing dinner by the waterfront.

Day 2: Kingston Historical Sites

• Morning: Tour the Frontenac County Schools Museum to understand the local education system during Jane's childhood.

---

1. https://www.thecanadianencyclopedia.ca/en/article/canada-west

- Afternoon: Visit Bellevue House, the former home of Sir John A. Macdonald, to learn about life in Canada West during the 1850s

Canada West | The Canadian Encyclopedia[2]

- EVENING: EXPLORE downtown Kingston and its historic architecture.

Day 3: Journey to Storrington, Ontario

- Morning: Travel to Storrington and visit the Storrington Presbyterian Church, where Jane might have worshipped

How to plan a successful genealogy research trip - MyHeritage Wiki[3]

- AFTERNOON: EXPLORE local archives and historical societies for records from the 1860s.

- Evening: Stay overnight in a local bed and breakfast.

Day 4: Exploring Ancestral Roots

- Morning: Visit local cemeteries to search for Jane's gravesite or any family markers.

- Afternoon: Meet with a local genealogist to discuss findings and gather more information.

- Evening: Return to Kingston and prepare for the next day's activities.

Day 5: Historical Sites in Canada West

---

2. https://www.thecanadianencyclopedia.ca/en/article/canada-west

3. https://www.myheritage.com/wiki/How_to_plan_a_successful_genealogy_research_trip

- Morning: Visit Upper Canada Village, a living history museum that recreates life in the 1860s.

- Afternoon: Explore the village and participate in hands-on activities to experience daily life as Jane might have known it.

- Evening: Return to Kingston for a relaxing evening.

Day 6: Reflect and Explore

- Morning: Take a scenic drive around the area, visiting any other historical sites or landmarks.

- Afternoon: Visit the Royal Military College of Canada to learn about its history and significance during Jane's time

Canada West | The Canadian Encyclopedia[4]

- EVENING: ENJOY A farewell dinner in Kingston.

Day 7: Departure

- Morning: Reflect on your journey and gather any final records or souvenirs.

- Afternoon: Depart from Kingston, Ontario.

This itinerary combines historical research with cultural experiences, making it a meaningful trip to honour Jane Smith's legacy.

---

4. https://www.thecanadianencyclopedia.ca/en/article/canada-west

CHARLES SMITH

CHARLES SMITH[6]

Charles Smith was born in Canada West (now Ontario) in 1860, a time when the region was undergoing significant growth and development as part of British North America.

Life in Canada West in 1860:

Economic Growth: Agriculture was the backbone of the economy, but towns and cities were growing with industries like timber and milling.

Transportation: The Grand Trunk Railway was expanding, improving transportation and connecting communities.

Education: Access to education was increasing with the establishment of public schools, though it often depended on location and family resources.

AS AN INFANT IN 1860, Charles would have been cared for in a family-centered environment, benefiting from the stability of a rural or small-town life in Canada West.

IN 1861, CHARLES SMITH, at just 1 year old, was living with his family in Storrington, Ontario, and identified as Presbyterian.

Life in Storrington, Ontario in 1861:

Community: Storrington was a rural township in Canada West, where agriculture dominated daily life. Neighbors often supported one another through shared religious and social activities.

Presbyterian Influence: As Presbyterians, the Smith family likely attended regular church services, which were central to their community and moral education.

Family Life: For a toddler like Charles, life revolved around the home, where older siblings and extended family played a big role in his upbringing.

THIS WAS A PERIOD OF simplicity and hard work, with families in Storrington maintaining close-knit ties and resilience in their rural environment.

GENEALOGY ITINERARY:

Day 1: Arrival in Kingston, Ontario

• Morning: Arrive in Kingston and check into your hotel.

• Afternoon: Visit the Kingston Penitentiary Museum to learn about the history of the area during the mid-19th century

https://bing.com/search?q=historical+sites+in+Canada+West+related+to+1860&form=SI

• EVENING: ENJOY A relaxing dinner by the waterfront.

Day 2: Kingston Historical Sites

- Morning: Tour the Frontenac County Schools Museum to understand the local education system during Charles's childhood.

- Afternoon: Visit Bellevue House, the former home of Sir John A. Macdonald, to learn about life in Canada West during the 1860s

https://bing.com/search?q=historical+sites+in+Canada+West+related+to+1860&form=SKPI

- EVENING: EXPLORE downtown Kingston and its historic architecture.

Day 3: Journey to Storrington, Ontario

- Morning: Travel to Storrington and visit the Storrington Presbyterian Church, where Charles might have worshipped.

- AFTERNOON: EXPLORE local archives and historical societies for records from the 1860s.

- Evening: Stay overnight in a local bed and breakfast.

Day 4: Exploring Ancestral Roots

- Morning: Visit local cemeteries to search for Charles's gravesite or any family markers.

- Afternoon: Meet with a local genealogist to discuss findings and gather more information.

- Evening: Return to Kingston and prepare for the next day's activities.

Day 5: Historical Sites in Canada West

- Morning: Visit Upper Canada Village, a living history museum that recreates life in the 1860s

Upper Canada Village[1]

- AFTERNOON: EXPLORE the village and participate in hands-on activities to experience daily life as Charles might have known it.

- Evening: Return to Kingston for a relaxing evening.

Day 6: Reflect and Explore

- Morning: Take a scenic drive around the area, visiting any other historical sites or landmarks.

- Afternoon: Visit the Royal Military College of Canada to learn about its history and significance during Charles's time

https://bing.com/search?q=historical+sites+in+Canada+West+related+to+1860&form=

- EVENING: ENJOY A farewell dinner in Kingston.

Day 7: Departure

- Morning: Reflect on your journey and gather any final records or souvenirs.

- Afternoon: Depart from Kingston, Ontario.

This itinerary combines historical research with cultural experiences, making it a meaningful trip to honor Charles Smith's legacy.

---

1. https://www.uppercanadavillage.com/

MARY (UNKNOWN) JOHNSTON

M ARY (UNKNOWN) JOHNSTON[7]

Mary Johnston was born in Ireland in 1801. Her maiden name is not currently known.

Life in Ireland in 1801:

Union with Britain: The year marked the establishment of the United Kingdom of Great Britain and Ireland under the Acts of Union. This political change created tensions among the Irish population, particularly Catholics, as it promised but failed to deliver greater equality.

Economy: Predominantly rural, Ireland's economy was based on agriculture. Many families relied on subsistence farming and faced challenges such as poor harvests and economic instability.

Daily Life: For Mary's family, life likely centered on maintaining their farm or trade. Traditional Irish customs, language, and religious practices were integral to the culture despite increasing British influence.

MARY'S UPBRINGING IN this transitional period shaped her resilience, which would serve her well if she emigrated or faced similar hardships later in life.

WHEN MARY JOHNSTON was 6 years old in 1807, Robert Fulton built the first commercially successful steamboat, the Clermont.

Significance of the Event:

The Clermont revolutionized water transportation, making it faster and more efficient, particularly on rivers and canals.

This advancement marked the early stages of the Industrial Revolution's influence on transportation, which would eventually impact trade and migration patterns, including those of Irish emigrants seeking opportunities abroad.

FOR MARY, LIVING IN rural Ireland, the event may not have had an immediate impact, but such technological progress hinted at the changes and opportunities emerging in the wider world during her lifetime.

WHEN MARY JOHNSTON was 25 years old in 1826, John Walker, an English chemist, invented the first friction match, revolutionizing how people started fires.

Significance of the Event:

Matches made lighting fires quicker and more convenient compared to traditional flint-and-steel or fire-starting methods.

This invention played a significant role in everyday life, from cooking to heating homes, especially in rural areas like Ireland, where Mary lived.

WHILE MARY MAY NOT have had immediate access to this innovation, its eventual widespread availability simplified domestic life during the 19th century.

WHEN MARY JOHNSTON was 38 years old in 1839, the Irish Hurricane struck Ireland, causing widespread devastation.

Significance of the Event:

This powerful storm, sometimes called "The Night of the Big Wind," hit Ireland on January 6-7, 1839, with hurricane-force winds that flattened homes, uprooted trees, and caused severe flooding.

It was one of the most destructive storms in Ireland's history, leaving thousands homeless and causing significant economic hardship.

Many people believed it was a sign of divine punishment or an omen, as it occurred shortly after New Year's Day, a time of reflection and renewal.

FOR SOMEONE LIKE MARY, this event would have been deeply impactful, particularly if she still had family or connections in Ireland. Even for those who had emigrated, the storm was a stark reminder of the challenges their homeland faced.

AT 44 YEARS OLD IN 1845, Mary Johnston witnessed the beginning of the Great Irish Famine, a catastrophic event that led to mass immigration from Ireland.

Impact of the Irish Famine:

The potato blight that caused widespread crop failures began in 1845, devastating the primary food source for much of Ireland's population.

Over the following years, famine conditions worsened, leading to mass starvation, disease, and emigration.

Many Irish families, desperate to escape the dire conditions, emigrated to places like Canada, the United States, and Australia.

CONNECTION TO MARY Johnston:

If Mary had already emigrated to Canada, she may have experienced an influx of Irish immigrants in her community. These immigrants brought stories of the famine's horrors, which would have been poignant and possibly heartbreaking for Mary, especially if she still had loved ones in Ireland.

This event marked a significant shift in Irish history and deeply influenced Irish communities abroad, including those in Upper Canada where Mary lived.

BY 1861, AT THE AGE of 60, Mary Johnston was a widow, practicing as an Anglican, and living in Storrington, Ontario.

Life in 1861 Storrington, Ontario:

Community Life: Storrington was a rural township with a mix of settlers, including Irish immigrants like Mary, who contributed to its cultural fabric.

Religion: As an Anglican, Mary would have attended the local Anglican Church, which served as a spiritual and social hub for the community.

Widowhood: As a widow, she likely relied on family, neighbors, or church support for companionship and assistance, especially in an era when widows often faced financial or social challenges.

BY THIS TIME, MARY would have seen Storrington grow as settlers cleared more land for farming and built roads to connect the township to neighboring areas. The Irish famine of the 1840s and ongoing immigration might have brought new faces to the township, adding to its development.

GENEALOGY ITINERARY:

Day 1: Arrival in Dublin, Ireland

- Morning: Arrive in Dublin and check into your hotel.

- Afternoon: Visit the National Archives of Ireland to explore records from the early 1800s.

- Evening: Enjoy a traditional Irish dinner at a local pub.

Day 2: Dublin Historical Sites

- Morning: Tour Dublin Castle, which has a rich history dating back to the 13th century

Ireland's Most Scenic Historic Sites | Historical Landmarks | History Hit[1]

- AFTERNOON: VISIT St. Patrick's Cathedral, an important Anglican site with a history dating back to the 12th century

---

1. https://www.historyhit.com/guides/historic-sites-in-ireland/

Ireland's Most Scenic Historic Sites | Historical Landmarks | History Hit[2]

- EVENING: STROLL ALONG the River Liffey and enjoy the vibrant city life.

Day 3: Journey to County Cork

- Morning: Travel to County Cork, where many Irish emigrants originated.

- Afternoon: Visit Blarney Castle and kiss the famous Blarney Stone

Ireland's Most Scenic Historic Sites | Historical Landmarks | History Hit[3]

- EVENING: EXPLORE the local countryside and stay overnight in a charming bed and breakfast.

Day 4: Exploring Ancestral Roots

- Morning: Visit local churches and cemeteries to search for any records or gravesites that might be connected to Mary's family.

- Afternoon: Meet with a local genealogist to discuss findings and gather more information.

- Evening: Return to Dublin and prepare for your flight to Canada.

Day 5: Arrival in Kingston, Ontario

- Morning: Arrive in Kingston, Ontario, and check into your hotel.

---

2. https://www.historyhit.com/guides/historic-sites-in-ireland/

3. https://www.historyhit.com/guides/historic-sites-in-ireland/

- Afternoon: Visit the Frontenac County Schools Museum to understand the local history of the area where Mary lived.

- Evening: Enjoy a relaxing evening by the waterfront.

Day 6: Storrington, Ontario

- Morning: Travel to Storrington and visit the local Anglican church, where Mary might have worshipped

Our Lady of England – Storrington and District Museum[4]

- AFTERNOON: EXPLORE local archives and historical societies for records from the 1860s.

- Evening: Visit local landmarks and enjoy the serene countryside.

Day 7: Reflect and Explore

- Morning: Visit local cemeteries to find Mary's gravesite or any family markers.

- Afternoon: Take a scenic drive around the area, visiting any other historical sites or landmarks.

- Evening: Return to Kingston for a farewell dinner.

Day 8: Departure

- Morning: Reflect on your journey and gather any final records or souvenirs.

- Afternoon: Depart from Kingston, Ontario.

---

4. https://storringtonmuseum.com/lady-of-england-by-simon-mole/

This itinerary combines historical research with cultural experiences, making it a meaningful trip to honor Mary Johnston's legacy

CHARLES SMITH

CHARLES SMITH[8]

Charles Smith was born in Ireland in 1836, a time of significant social and political developments.

Life in Ireland in 1836:

Agrarian Economy: The majority of Ireland's population depended on agriculture, with tenant farming being the dominant way of life. Potatoes were the staple food for many families.

Tensions and Reforms: The Irish Tithe War (1830–1836) had recently ended, a conflict where tenant farmers protested against paying tithes to the Anglican Church. These events highlighted the growing discontent among Catholics regarding economic and social inequalities.

Immigration Trends: Economic hardship and limited opportunities were already driving some Irish families to consider emigration, though the Great Famine was still nearly a decade away.

Social Life: Family and community ties were strong, with a rich cultural life that included traditional music, dance, and storytelling.

CHARLES'S EARLY YEARS in Ireland likely involved a life centered on rural traditions and challenges before he or his family eventually made the journey to Canada.

CHARLES SMITH WAS 9 years old in 1845 during the Irish immigration caused by the Great Famine.

The Great Famine and Irish Immigration:

The Famine's Start: A devastating potato blight began in 1845, causing widespread starvation and hardship in Ireland, where potatoes were the primary food source for many families.

Mass Emigration: That year marked the beginning of a massive wave of emigration as Irish families sought refuge and opportunities abroad, particularly in North America, including Canada.

Conditions for Emigrants: Many emigrants faced perilous voyages on overcrowded ships, later called "coffin ships" due to high mortality rates caused by disease and malnutrition.

Impact in Canada: Irish immigrants became a significant part of Canadian society, contributing to the labor force and establishing communities while enduring prejudice and hardship.

AT THIS TIME, CHARLES would have witnessed or experienced the struggles and decisions families faced as they sought a better life abroad.

IN 1861, CHARLES SMITH was 25 years old, working as a farmer, and practicing the Presbyterian faith while residing in Storrington, Ontario.

Life in Storrington, Ontario, in 1861:

Agricultural Focus: Farming was a dominant occupation in the region, with settlers like Charles working the land to sustain their families

ECHOES OF STORRINGTON

and contribute to the growing agricultural economy of Canada West (modern-day Ontario).

Community Life: Presbyterianism was a significant faith tradition in the area, shaping community practices and providing a sense of identity and support for settlers, particularly those of Irish and Scottish descent.

Rural Living: Life in rural Storrington required hard work and resourcefulness, with families growing crops, raising livestock, and relying on local networks for trade and assistance.

CHARLES WOULD HAVE been part of a modest but resilient community, navigating the challenges of rural life while contributing to the economic and social fabric of the township.

GENEALOGY ITINERARY:

Day 1: Arrival in Dublin, Ireland

- Morning: Arrive in Dublin and check into your hotel.

- Afternoon: Visit the National Archives of Ireland to explore records from the 1830s.

- Evening: Enjoy a traditional Irish dinner at a local pub.

Day 2: Dublin Historical Sites

- Morning: Tour Dublin Castle, which has a rich history dating back to the 13th century

Ireland's Most Scenic Historic Sites | Historical Landmarks | History Hit[1]

---

1. https://www.historyhit.com/guides/historic-sites-in-ireland/

- AFTERNOON: VISIT St. Patrick's Cathedral, an important site for the Anglican community with a history dating back to the 12th century

Ireland's Most Scenic Historic Sites | Historical Landmarks | History Hit[2]

- EVENING: STROLL ALONG the River Liffey and enjoy the vibrant city life.

Day 3: Journey to County Cork

- Morning: Travel to County Cork, where many Irish emigrants originated.

- Afternoon: Visit Blarney Castle and kiss the famous Blarney Stone

Ireland's Most Scenic Historic Sites | Historical Landmarks | History Hit[3]

- EVENING: EXPLORE the local countryside and stay overnight in a charming bed and breakfast.

Day 4: Exploring Ancestral Roots

- Morning: Visit local churches and cemeteries to search for any records or gravesites that might be connected to Charles's family.

---

2. https://www.historyhit.com/guides/historic-sites-in-ireland/

3. https://www.historyhit.com/guides/historic-sites-in-ireland/

- Afternoon: Meet with a local genealogist to discuss findings and gather more information.

- Evening: Return to Dublin and prepare for your flight to Canada.

Day 5: Arrival in Kingston, Ontario

- Morning: Arrive in Kingston, Ontario, and check into your hotel.

- Afternoon: Visit the Frontenac County Schools Museum to understand the local history of the area where Charles lived.

- Evening: Enjoy a relaxing evening by the waterfront.

Day 6: Storrington, Ontario

- Morning: Travel to Storrington and visit the Storrington Presbyterian Church, where Charles might have worshipped

https://www.archeion.ca/st-andrews-presbyterian-church-sunbury-ont

---

- AFTERNOON: EXPLORE local archives and historical societies for records from the 1860s.

- Evening: Visit local landmarks and enjoy the serene countryside.

Day 7: Reflect and Explore

- Morning: Visit local cemeteries to find Charles's gravesite or any family markers.

- Afternoon: Take a scenic drive around the area, visiting any other historical sites or landmarks.

- Evening: Return to Kingston for a farewell dinner.

Day 8: Departure

- Morning: Reflect on your journey and gather any final records or souvenirs.

- Afternoon: Depart from Kingston, Ontario.

This itinerary combines historical research with cultural experiences, making it a meaningful trip to honor Charles Smith's legacy.

CAROLINE (UNKNOWN) SMITH

CAROLINE (UNKNOWN) SMITH[9]

Caroline, born in 1837 in Upper Canada, was the wife of Charles Smith. While her maiden name remains unknown, her birth during this period places her within a time of significant transformation in Canadian history.

Life in Upper Canada in 1837:

Political Unrest: Caroline was born in the same year as the Upper Canada Rebellion, a period of political instability and calls for reform in colonial governance.

Rural Life: Families in Upper Canada were largely engaged in agriculture or small-scale trades, with communities growing around farming settlements and trading posts.

Education and Roles: As a woman, Caroline likely received limited formal education, with her upbringing focusing on domestic skills and community roles, typical for women of her era.

HER LATER MARRIAGE to Charles Smith would align her with the Presbyterian community of Storrington, Ontario, as they built their lives together in a farming household.

CAROLINE WAS 11 YEARS old in 1848 when the principle of responsible government was established in British North America. This milestone shifted political power from appointed colonial governors to elected representatives, laying the foundation for modern democracy in Canada.

At the time, Caroline would have been growing up in a rural Upper Canada setting, where political reforms may have had limited direct impact on daily life but signaled a period of increasing autonomy and progress for the colony.

IN 1861, CAROLINE, at 24 years old, was married, Presbyterian, and living in Storrington, Ontario. As a young wife during this period, her life likely revolved around managing household responsibilities, supporting her husband's farming work, and participating in the local Presbyterian community.

Ontario's rural life in the mid-19th century was marked by hard work and strong community ties, with families often relying on one another for labor and social connection. The Presbyterian faith would have provided both spiritual guidance and a social framework for her and her family.

GENEALOGY ITINERARY:

Day 1: Arrival in Kingston, Ontario

- Morning: Arrive in Kingston and check into your hotel.

- Afternoon: Visit the Kingston Penitentiary Museum to learn about the history of the area during the mid-19th century

Rebellion in Upper Canada | The Canadian Encyclopedia[1]

---

1. https://www.thecanadianencyclopedia.ca/en/article/rebellion-in-upper-canada

- EVENING: ENJOY A relaxing dinner by the waterfront.

Day 2: Kingston Historical Sites

- Morning: Tour the Frontenac County Schools Museum to understand the local education system during Caroline's childhood.

- Afternoon: Visit Bellevue House, the former home of Sir John A. Macdonald, to learn about life in Upper Canada during the 1830s

Rebellion in Upper Canada | The Canadian Encyclopedia[2]

- EVENING: EXPLORE downtown Kingston and its historic architecture.

Day 3: Journey to Storrington, Ontario

- Morning: Travel to Storrington and visit the Storrington Presbyterian Church, where Caroline might have worshipped

How to plan a successful genealogy research trip - MyHeritage Wiki[3]

- AFTERNOON: EXPLORE local archives and historical societies for records from the 1860s.

- Evening: Stay overnight in a local bed and breakfast.

Day 4: Exploring Ancestral Roots

- Morning: Visit local cemeteries to search for Caroline's gravesite or any family markers.

---

2. https://www.thecanadianencyclopedia.ca/en/article/rebellion-in-upper-canada

3. https://www.myheritage.com/wiki/How_to_plan_a_successful_genealogy_research_trip

- Afternoon: Meet with a local genealogist to discuss findings and gather more information.

- Evening: Return to Kingston and prepare for the next day's activities.

Day 5: Historical Sites in Upper Canada

- Morning: Visit Upper Canada Village, a living history museum that recreates life in the 1860s

1837-1838 - Canadian Military Heritage Project[4]

- AFTERNOON: EXPLORE the village and participate in hands-on activities to experience daily life as Caroline might have known it.

- Evening: Return to Kingston for a relaxing evening.

Day 6: Reflect and Explore

- Morning: Take a scenic drive around the area, visiting any other historical sites or landmarks.

- Afternoon: Visit the Royal Military College of Canada to learn about its history and significance during Caroline's time

Rebellion in Upper Canada | The Canadian Encyclopedia[5]

- EVENING: ENJOY A farewell dinner in Kingston.

Day 7: Departure

---

4. https://canadianmilitaryproject.com/1837-rebellion/

5. https://www.thecanadianencyclopedia.ca/en/article/rebellion-in-upper-canada

- Morning: Reflect on your journey and gather any final records or souvenirs.

- Afternoon: Depart from Kingston, Ontario.

This itinerary combines historical research with cultural experiences, making it a meaningful trip to honor Caroline Smith's legacy.

ELIZEBETH SMITH

ELIZEBETH SMITH[10]

Elizebeth Smith, born in Canada West (modern-day Ontario) in 1856, was the daughter of Charles Smith and his wife Caroline. Her childhood was shaped by life in rural Ontario during a time of growth and change in the region. Families like hers typically relied on farming and lived closely connected to their communities and church. As the child of Presbyterian parents, faith likely played a central role in her upbringing.

IN 1861, ELIZEBETH Smith was 5 years old, living with her family in Storrington, Ontario. She was listed as Presbyterian, reflecting the strong religious traditions of her household. Storrington was a rural community, and Elizebeth likely spent her early years surrounded by the natural beauty of the Canadian countryside, helping with small chores around the farm and participating in family and community activities centered on faith and rural life.

GENEALOGY ITINERARY:

Day 1: Arrival in Kingston, Ontario

- Morning: Arrive in Kingston and check into your hotel.

- Afternoon: Visit the Kingston Penitentiary Museum to learn about the history of the area during the mid-19th century

Heritage Colchester[1]

---

1. https://heritagecolchester.ca/

- EVENING: ENJOY A relaxing dinner by the waterfront.

Day 2: Kingston Historical Sites

- Morning: Tour the Frontenac County Schools Museum to understand the local education system during Elizabeth's childhood.

- Afternoon: Visit Bellevue House, the former home of Sir John A. Macdonald, to learn about life in Canada West during the 1850s

Heritage Colchester[2]

- EVENING: EXPLORE downtown Kingston and its historic architecture.

Day 3: Journey to Storrington, Ontario

- Morning: Travel to Storrington and visit the Storrington Presbyterian Church, where Elizabeth might have worshipped

Place:Storrington, Frontenac, Ontario, Canada - Genealogy[3]

- AFTERNOON: EXPLORE local archives and historical societies for records from the 1860s.

- Evening: Stay overnight in a local bed and breakfast.

Day 4: Exploring Ancestral Roots

---

2. https://heritagecolchester.ca/

3. https://www.werelate.org/wiki/Place:Storrington%2C_Frontenac%2C_Ontario%2C_Canada

- Morning: Visit local cemeteries to search for Elizebeth's gravesite or any family markers.

- Afternoon: Meet with a local genealogist to discuss findings and gather more information.

- Evening: Return to Kingston and prepare for the next day's activities.

Day 5: Historical Sites in Canada West

- Morning: Visit Upper Canada Village, a living history museum that recreates life in the 1860s

1856 in Canada - Wikipedia[4]

- AFTERNOON: EXPLORE the village and participate in hands-on activities to experience daily life as Elizebeth might have known it.

- Evening: Return to Kingston for a relaxing evening.

Day 6: Reflect and Explore

- Morning: Take a scenic drive around the area, visiting any other historical sites or landmarks.

- Afternoon: Visit the Royal Military College of Canada to learn about its history and significance during Elizebeth's time

Heritage Colchester[5]

- EVENING: ENJOY A farewell dinner in Kingston.

---

4. https://en.wikipedia.org/wiki/1856_in_Canada

5. https://heritagecolchester.ca/

Day 7: Departure

- Morning: Reflect on your journey and gather any final records or souvenirs.

- Afternoon: Depart from Kingston, Ontario.

This itinerary combines historical research with cultural experiences, making it a meaningful trip to honour Elizebeth Smith's legacy.

SIMEON SMITH

SIMEON SMITH[11]

Simeon Smith, son of Charles and Caroline Smith, was born in Canada West in 1858. He grew up in a rural setting where farming and community life were central to daily living. At this time, Canada West (now Ontario) was undergoing economic growth and development, with railroads expanding and agriculture thriving. Simeon's early years would have been shaped by these changes and the close-knit environment of his family and community.

IN 1861, SIMEON SMITH was 3 years old, Presbyterian, and living with his family in Storrington, Ontario. At this young age, he was likely surrounded by the rhythms of rural life, with his parents, Charles and Caroline, working as farmers. Storrington's close-knit community and agricultural setting provided a structured and faith-centered environment for families like the Smiths.

GENEALOGY ITINERARY:

DAY 1: ARRIVAL IN ONTARIO

- Destination: Kingston, Ontario
- Activities:
- Check into a local hotel or bed and breakfast.

- Visit the Kingston Historical Society to gather preliminary information and resources about the region during the mid-19th century.

Day 2: Exploring Storrington

- Destination: Storrington, Ontario

- Activities:

- Visit the local archives or library to search for records related to Simeon Smith and his family.

- Explore the area to get a sense of the landscape and environment where Simeon grew up.

- Visit local Presbyterian churches to inquire about historical records and possibly view the church where Simeon and his family might have worshipped.

Day 3: Historical Research and Records

- Destination: Storrington, Ontario

- Activities:

- Spend the day at the local archives or library, focusing on census records, land records, and any other documents that might provide insights into Simeon's early life.

- Meet with local historians or genealogy groups to discuss your findings and get additional leads.

Day 4: Visiting Cemeteries and Historical Sites

- Destination: Storrington, Ontario

- Activities:

- Visit local cemeteries to find the gravesites of Simeon Smith and his family members.

- Explore historical sites and landmarks in the area to understand the context of Simeon's life in the 1860s.

Day 5: Day Trip to Nearby Historical Locations

- Destination: Surrounding areas of Storrington

- Activities:

- Take a day trip to nearby towns and villages to explore additional archives, libraries, and historical societies.

- Visit any relevant museums or heritage sites that provide a broader understanding of life in Canada West during the 19th century.

Day 6: Reflection and Documentation

- Destination: Kingston, Ontario

- Activities:

- Return to Kingston to compile and document your findings.

- Visit the Kingston Frontenac Public Library for any final research and to use their genealogy resources.

- Reflect on the journey and prepare a summary of your discoveries to share with family members.

Day 7: Departure

- Destination: Home

- Activities:

- Check out of your accommodation and travel back home.

- Plan a family gathering to share the stories and information you uncovered about Simeon Smith.

MARGARET SMITH

MARGARET SMITH[12]

In 1859, when Margaret Smith was born in Canada West, life was defined by a mix of agricultural traditions, colonial expansion, and technological innovation. Canada West (now Ontario) was predominantly rural, with farming communities serving as the backbone of society. Settlers focused on cultivating the land and creating self-sustaining households. The railway system was expanding, connecting towns and cities, which facilitated trade and communication.

Politically, tensions were growing in the Province of Canada as debates about representation and governance intensified, laying the groundwork for eventual Confederation in 1867. Internationally, the industrial revolution continued to transform societies, and in Canada, the seeds of modernization were taking root with advances in transportation and industry.

For families like the Smiths, faith and community played a central role. Presbyterianism provided spiritual guidance and a sense of belonging, while daily life revolved around farming, household duties, and navigating the challenges of rural existence.

IN 1861, MARGARET SMITH was a 2-year-old living in Storrington, Ontario with her Presbyterian family. Life in Storrington was rural and community-oriented, with most families like hers relying on agriculture for their livelihood. Margaret would have been surrounded by a close-knit network of relatives and neighbors who worked together to sustain their farms.

As a toddler, she would have been cared for in a household where faith, hard work, and tradition were key values. The Presbyterian Church would have been a central part of family and community life, shaping their social and moral framework. Her family likely participated in church services, community events, and seasonal activities tied to farming, such as planting and harvest.

Life in 1861 was also marked by Canada's growing population, infrastructure improvements like roads and railways, and the ongoing discussions about governance that would eventually lead to Canadian Confederation.

GENEALOGY ITINERARY:

Day 1: Arrival in Ontario

• Destination: Kingston, Ontario

• Activities:

• Check into a local hotel or bed and breakfast.

• Visit the Kingston Historical Society to gather preliminary information and resources about the region during the mid-19th century.

Day 2: Exploring Storrington

• Destination: Storrington, Ontario

• Activities:

• Visit the local archives or library to search for records related to Margaret Smith and her family.

- Explore the area to get a sense of the landscape and environment where Margaret grew up.

- Visit local Presbyterian churches to inquire about historical records and possibly view the church where Margaret and her family might have worshipped.

Day 3: Historical Research and Records

- Destination: Storrington, Ontario

- Activities:

- Spend the day at the local archives or library, focusing on census records, land records, and any other documents that might provide insights into Margaret's early life.

- Meet with local historians or genealogy groups to discuss your findings and get additional leads.

Day 4: Visiting Cemeteries and Historical Sites

- Destination: Storrington, Ontario

- Activities:

- Visit local cemeteries to find gravesites of Margaret Smith and her family members.

- Explore historical sites and landmarks in the area to understand the context of Margaret's life in the 1860s.

Day 5: Day Trip to Nearby Historical Locations

- Destination: Surrounding areas of Storrington

- Activities:

- Take a day trip to nearby towns and villages to explore additional archives, libraries, and historical societies.

- Visit any relevant museums or heritage sites that provide a broader understanding of life in Canada West during the 19th century.

Day 6: Reflection and Documentation

- Destination: Kingston, Ontario

- Activities:

- Return to Kingston to compile and document your findings.

- Visit the Kingston Frontenac Public Library for any final research and to use their genealogy resources.

- Reflect on the journey and prepare a summary of your discoveries to share with family members.

Day 7: Departure

- Destination: Home

- Activities:

- Check out of your accommodation and travel back home.

- Plan a family gathering to share the stories and information you uncovered about Margaret Smith.

CORNEUS SMITH

CORNEUS SMITH[13]

Corneus Smith was born in Ireland in 1796, a time of significant upheaval and change. Ireland was experiencing the effects of the Irish Rebellion of 1798, which was influenced by revolutionary movements in France and America. Tensions between the Protestant Ascendancy and the largely Catholic population were escalating, contributing to a volatile political and social environment.

Economically, much of Ireland was still agrarian, with tenant farmers working on land owned by wealthy landlords. The rural poor often faced challenging conditions, relying on potatoes as a staple crop, a dependency that would later have devastating consequences during the Great Famine.

The late 18th century also saw the beginnings of industrialization in Britain, which was slowly making its way to Ireland, although rural areas remained largely untouched by these changes. In this environment, Corneus would have been born into a society deeply shaped by tradition but on the cusp of modernization and political reform.

CORNEUS SMITH WAS 21 years old when the bicycle was invented in 1817. Known as the Draisine or "running machine," it was created by Karl von Drais in Germany. This early bicycle had no pedals, requiring the rider to push off the ground with their feet. It was a novel innovation that marked the beginning of modern transportation beyond walking or using animals.

At the time, technological advancements were starting to influence daily life, and inventions like the Draisine hinted at a future where mobility and efficiency would be significantly enhanced. While Corneus likely wouldn't have encountered a Draisine in Ireland, its invention symbolized the growing ingenuity of the Industrial Age.

CORNEUS SMITH WAS 49 years old during the Irish Immigration of 1845, a direct result of the Great Irish Famine (1845–1852). The famine, caused by a potato blight, devastated Ireland, leading to widespread starvation and the displacement of millions. Many Irish families fled to North America, particularly Canada and the United States, in search of survival and better opportunities.

If Corneus lived in Ireland at the time, he would have witnessed the severe hardships of the famine—food shortages, evictions, and mass emigration. For those who left, the journey across the Atlantic was perilous, often aboard overcrowded and poorly equipped "coffin ships." Those who stayed faced immense struggles, trying to adapt to declining resources and economic instability.

Irish Immigration significantly influenced Canada's demographics, particularly in Ontario and Quebec, where many Irish settlers established communities that contributed to the country's cultural fabric.

CORNEUS SMITH WAS 50 years old in 1846 when the sewing machine was patented by Elias Howe. This invention revolutionized the textile and clothing industries, dramatically improving the efficiency of producing garments.

If Corneus had immigrated to Canada by this time, he might have heard of this breakthrough, especially in towns and cities where tailors and textile workers operated. For individuals and families, the sewing machine eventually made its way into homes, enabling faster repairs and creation of clothing—a significant improvement for working-class households striving to maintain their wardrobes affordably. This invention marked the beginning of industrialized fashion and influenced economic and social life across North America.

IN 1861, CORNEUS SMITH was 65 years old, single, and Presbyterian, residing in Storrington, Ontario. By this time, Storrington was a rural township characterized by its farming communities and close-knit social structures. As a single man in his mid-sixties, Corneus likely participated in the local economy through farming or other labor-intensive work, which was common for men of his age and background.

Living in Storrington during this period meant dealing with the challenges and opportunities of rural Ontario life, such as reliance on agriculture, navigating harsh winters, and participating in the Presbyterian church, which was a central institution for spiritual guidance and community events. The census of 1861 reflects a growing settlement in the area, with many Irish immigrants and their descendants contributing to the cultural and economic fabric of the region.

GENEALOGY ITINERARY:

Day 1: Arrival in Ontario

- Destination: Kingston, Ontario
- Activities:

- Check into a local hotel or bed and breakfast.

- Visit the Kingston Historical Society to gather preliminary information and resources about the region during the mid-19th century.

Day 2: Exploring Storrington

- Destination: Storrington, Ontario

- Activities:

- Visit the local archives or library to search for records related to Corneus Smith and his family.

- Explore the area to get a sense of the landscape and environment where Corneus lived.

- Visit local Presbyterian churches to inquire about historical records and possibly view the church where Corneus and his family might have worshipped.

Day 3: Historical Research and Records

- Destination: Storrington, Ontario

- Activities:

- Spend the day at the local archives or library, focusing on census records, land records, and any other documents that might provide insights into Corneus's life.

- Meet with local historians or genealogy groups to discuss your findings and get additional leads.

Day 4: Visiting Cemeteries and Historical Sites

- Destination: Storrington, Ontario

- Activities:

- Visit local cemeteries to find gravesites of Corneus Smith and his family members.

- Explore historical sites and landmarks in the area to understand the context of Corneus's life in the 1860s.

Day 5: Day Trip to Nearby Historical Locations

- Destination: Surrounding areas of Storrington

- Activities:

- Take a day trip to nearby towns and villages to explore additional archives, libraries, and historical societies.

- Visit any relevant museums or heritage sites that provide a broader understanding of life in Canada West during the 19th century.

Day 6: Reflection and Documentation

- Destination: Kingston, Ontario

- Activities:

- Return to Kingston to compile and document your findings.

- Visit the Kingston Frontenac Public Library for any final research and to use their genealogy resources.

- Reflect on the journey and prepare a summary of your discoveries to share with family members.

Day 7: Departure

- Destination: Home

- Activities:

- Check out of your accommodation and travel back home.

- Plan a family gathering to share the stories and information you uncovered about Corneus Smith.

JAMES SMITH

J**AMES SMITH**[14]

James Smith was born in 1831 in Ireland, a period marked by social and economic challenges in the country. Ireland was undergoing significant change, with a population boom leading to widespread poverty in rural areas. Tenant farmers struggled under high rents and poor harvests, which foreshadowed the devastating Irish Famine of the 1840s. Politically, Daniel O'Connell's Catholic Emancipation movement had recently achieved its goal in 1829, leading to greater religious freedoms for Catholics.

For James's family, life likely revolved around agriculture, as most Irish families of the time depended on farming for their livelihoods. The social structure was deeply tied to the land, and emigration had not yet reached the massive scale it would during the famine years. Life would have been modest and challenging, but the Irish spirit of community and resilience shaped daily life.

JAMES SMITH WAS 8 YEARS old when the Irish Hurricane struck in 1839. This storm, one of the most severe ever to hit Ireland, caused widespread destruction, particularly in southern and eastern regions. Known for its strong winds and torrential rain, it led to severe flooding, uprooted trees, and significant damage to buildings and crops. The hurricane disrupted everyday life for many, adding to the hardships already faced by families in rural Ireland. For James and his family, this event would have been another challenge in a decade marked by economic difficulties and uncertainty, possibly leading to further contemplation of emigration.

JAMES SMITH WAS 14 years old during the Irish Immigration of 1845, a period marked by the beginning of the Great Famine. The Irish Famine, caused by a potato blight, led to mass starvation, disease, and extreme poverty, pushing many Irish families to seek better opportunities abroad. Over a million people died, and millions more emigrated, primarily to places like Canada, the United States, and Australia.

For James and his family, this was a pivotal time. The famine made life increasingly unbearable, and emigration to places like Canada West (modern-day Ontario) was seen as a lifeline. Many Irish immigrants faced harsh conditions on overcrowded ships during their journey, but once they arrived in Canada, they often found work on farms or in developing communities, contributing to the growth of places like Storrington, Ontario, where James would later settle. This period of hardship and migration had a profound impact on James' life and the future of his family in their new homeland.

IN 1861, JAMES SMITH was 30 years old, single, and living in Storrington, Ontario. As a Presbyterian farmer, James would have been part of a growing, rural community. At that time, Canada was transitioning from its colonial past into a more self-sufficient nation. The Confederation of Canada was still a few years away (1867), but changes were already underway in the agricultural and social fabric of the region.

Farmers like James were working the land, relying heavily on agriculture for both sustenance and income. Life on the farm would have been physically demanding, with long days dedicated to growing crops, raising livestock, and maintaining property. Tools and technology were beginning to evolve, but much of the work was still done by hand, with only a few innovations like the sewing machine (patented in 1846) gradually finding their way into rural homes.

The Presbyterian faith, a significant aspect of many early settlers' lives, would have been central to James' community life. Churches were not only places of worship but also served as social and communal gathering spots, where families like his would find support, fellowship, and a sense of belonging.

Given the backdrop of the Irish Immigration (1845-1852), James' parents or grandparents may have been among the Irish emigrants fleeing the Great Famine. His community would have included many others from Ireland, which influenced the local culture, including its religious practices. The farm life was often shared among family members, and James, being single, might have worked closely with other family members or had some freedom to focus on developing his own farmstead.

Overall, this period in Storrington, Ontario, was one of hard work, resilience, and community development as settlers continued to make their mark on the land and integrate into a changing world.

GENEALOGY ITINERARY:

Day 1: Arrival in Ontario

- Destination: Kingston, Ontario
- Activities:
- Check into a local hotel or bed and breakfast.

- Visit the Kingston Historical Society to gather preliminary information and resources about the region during the mid-19th century.

Day 2: Exploring Storrington

- Destination: Storrington, Ontario

- Activities:

- Visit the local archives or library to search for records related to James Smith and his farming activities.

- Explore the area to get a sense of the landscape and environment where James lived and worked.

- Visit local Presbyterian churches to inquire about historical records and possibly view the church where James might have worshipped.

Day 3: Historical Research and Records

- Destination: Storrington, Ontario

- Activities:

- Spend the day at the local archives or library, focusing on census records, land records, and any other documents that might provide insights into James's life as a farmer.

- Meet with local historians or genealogy groups to discuss your findings and get additional leads.

Day 4: Visiting Cemeteries and Historical Sites

- Destination: Storrington, Ontario

- Activities:

- Visit local cemeteries to find gravesites of James Smith and his family members.

- Explore historical sites and landmarks in the area to understand the context of James's life in the 1860s.

Day 5: Day Trip to Nearby Historical Locations

- Destination: Surrounding areas of Storrington

- Activities:

- Take a day trip to nearby towns and villages to explore additional archives, libraries, and historical societies.

- Visit any relevant museums or heritage sites that provide a broader understanding of life in Canada West during the 19th century.

Day 6: Reflection and Documentation

- Destination: Kingston, Ontario

- Activities:

- Return to Kingston to compile and document your findings.

- Visit the Kingston Frontenac Public Library for any final research and to use their genealogy resources.

- Reflect on the journey and prepare a summary of your discoveries to share with family members.

Day 7: Departure

- Destination: Home

- Activities:

- Check out of your accommodation and travel back home.

- Plan a family gathering to share the stories and information you uncovered about James Smith.

ROSEY SHAW

ROSEY SHAW[15]

Rosey Shaw was born in Ireland in 1831, a time when Ireland was experiencing significant social and political turmoil. This period marked the early years of the Great Irish Famine (1845–1852), which would later affect many Irish families. However, in 1831, Ireland was still under British rule, and its population was largely rural, with many people living in farming communities.

The early 1830s in Ireland saw social reforms such as the Act of Union (1801), which had already integrated Ireland into the United Kingdom, but tensions remained between the Irish population and British rule. This environment likely influenced many Irish families, who would later immigrate to places like Canada in search of better opportunities.

ROSEY SHAW WAS 8 YEARS old when the Irish Hurricane occurred in 1839. This devastating storm, which hit the Irish coast on October 6, 1839, was one of the most powerful and destructive storms ever to affect Ireland. It caused widespread flooding, property damage, and loss of life, particularly in areas like Dublin, Cork, and Wexford. The hurricane left a lasting impact on the Irish population, and many families were affected by its destruction.

At the time, Rosey and many others living in Ireland would have witnessed the aftermath of this severe weather event, which further compounded the hardships faced by the population. It likely added to the sense of uncertainty and hardship that many Irish families were already experiencing, particularly those living in rural areas.

ROSEY SHAW WAS 14 YEARS old when the Irish Immigration began in 1845, following the onset of the Great Irish Famine. The famine was caused by a potato blight that devastated crops, leading to widespread hunger and suffering across Ireland. Over the next several years, millions of Irish people were forced to emigrate in search of better opportunities, and many headed to places like North America, Australia, and Britain.

During this time, Rosey would have experienced the growing distress in Ireland as the famine worsened, with many families losing their livelihoods and struggling to survive. The mass migration would have dramatically reshaped the Irish diaspora, and many people, including likely Rosey's family, would have looked to Canada, the United States, and other destinations for hope, despite the difficulties and dangers of long sea voyages.

In 1845, the first wave of the Irish immigrants began arriving, marking a significant chapter in both Irish and Canadian history as settlers sought a new life away from the ravages of the famine.

IN 1861, ROSEY SHAW was 30 years old, single, and a Presbyterian living in Storrington, Ontario. At this time, Storrington was part of a growing, largely agricultural community, and many families in the area had settled there after immigrating from Ireland or Britain. The Presbyterian faith would have played a central role in her daily life, as it did for many of the settlers in Ontario, influencing both her social and community interactions.

Rosey would have likely lived a simple but hardworking life, possibly working on a farm or helping with household duties. The agricultural lifestyle meant that most people were involved in producing food, which was vital for survival, particularly during times when travel and communication with distant areas were limited. Life in rural Ontario could be challenging, especially for single women, who often had fewer opportunities outside of domestic work or helping family members on their land.

The 1861 census reflects a period of relative stability and growth in Canada West (now Ontario), with the population beginning to experience the benefits of the completion of the Grand Trunk Railway and the increasing settlement of immigrants from Ireland, Britain, and elsewhere. The effects of the Irish Famine had led to significant immigration, and Rosey would have been part of a generation of Irish immigrants contributing to the settlement and development of Ontario, particularly in rural areas like Storrington.

GENEALOGY ITINERARY:

Day 1: Arrival in Ontario

- Destination: Kingston, Ontario

- Activities:

- Check into a local hotel or bed and breakfast.

- Visit the Kingston Historical Society to gather preliminary information and resources about the region during the mid-19th century.

Day 2: Exploring Storrington

- Destination: Storrington, Ontario

- Activities:

- Visit the local archives or library to search for records related to Rosey Shaw and her family.

- Explore the area to get a sense of the landscape and environment where Rosey lived.

- Visit local Presbyterian churches to inquire about historical records and possibly view the church where Rosey might have worshipped.

Day 3: Historical Research and Records

- Destination: Storrington, Ontario

- Activities:

- Spend the day at the local archives or library, focusing on census records, land records, and any other documents that might provide insights into Rosey's life.

- Meet with local historians or genealogy groups to discuss your findings and get additional leads.

Day 4: Visiting Cemeteries and Historical Sites

- Destination: Storrington, Ontario

- Activities:

- Visit local cemeteries to find gravesites of Rosey Shaw and her family members.

- Explore historical sites and landmarks in the area to understand the context of Rosey's life in the 1860s.

Day 5: Day Trip to Nearby Historical Locations

- Destination: Surrounding areas of Storrington

- Activities:

- Take a day trip to nearby towns and villages to explore additional archives, libraries, and historical societies.

- Visit any relevant museums or heritage sites that provide a broader understanding of life in Canada West during the 19th century.

Day 6: Reflection and Documentation

- Destination: Kingston, Ontario

- Activities:

- Return to Kingston to compile and document your findings.

- Visit the Kingston Frontenac Public Library for any final research and to use their genealogy resources.

- Reflect on the journey and prepare a summary of your discoveries to share with family members.

Day 7: Departure

- Destination: Home

- Activities:

- Check out of your accommodation and travel back home.

- Plan a family gathering to share the stories and information you uncovered about Rosey Shaw.

WILLIAM STEWART

WILLIAM STEWART[16]

William Stewart was born in Upper Canada in 1833, during a period of significant change and development in the region. At the time, Upper Canada (which would later become Ontario) was a British colony, and the early 19th century marked the consolidation of British control and the expansion of settlement.

In the 1830s, Upper Canada was experiencing increasing immigration, especially from the British Isles, and was beginning to develop its infrastructure, including roads, canals, and early forms of industry. The population was growing, and agriculture was a major part of the economy, although tensions were rising in the colony, leading up to the Upper Canada Rebellion of 1837, which was a response to grievances related to political power, the influence of the Family Compact (an elite governing group), and lack of representation.

For someone like William Stewart, born in 1833, this would have been a time of uncertainty but also opportunity, as the colony was in the midst of laying the foundations for a prosperous future. Growing up in Upper Canada meant adjusting to the challenges of rural life, including farming, building community, and perhaps dealing with the tensions surrounding the rebellions of the 1830s. If William's family was part of the immigration wave from Britain or Ireland, he may have witnessed the effects of that migration, as many Irish and British settlers had arrived in Upper Canada to escape hardship, including the Irish famine.

By the time William was an adult, Upper Canada had already begun its transformation into the Province of Ontario after the establishment of the Province of Canada in 1841. The colony was beginning to modernize with the rise of transportation networks, and settlers were steadily populating the land, establishing farms and small towns.

WILLIAM STEWART, BORN in 1833, would have been only 4 years old during the Lower and Upper Canadian Rebellions of 1837. These rebellions were part of a larger movement for democratic reform in the British colonies. The rebellions were sparked by growing dissatisfaction with the colonial governments, which were seen as unresponsive to the needs of the people. In Upper Canada (now Ontario), the rebellion was led by William Lyon Mackenzie, who was advocating for more representative government and an end to the control held by the Family Compact, a small group of elites who dominated the political scene.

For a young child like William, life during this period would have been affected by the unrest around him. Although he was too young to understand the full scope of the events, the rebellions and the resulting crackdowns likely impacted his community. Families were torn between supporting the reformers and maintaining loyalty to the colonial government. The presence of military forces, the disruption of daily life, and the uncertainty of the time would have been felt by everyone in Upper Canada, even if they weren't directly involved in the conflict.

For many families in Upper Canada, including the Stewart family, the rebellion would have been a distant but unsettling presence. They would have witnessed the social and political upheaval, as well as the eventual military response, which included the harsh punishment of some of the rebels. Despite the failure of the rebellions to achieve immediate reform, they set the stage for later changes in the colony, leading to the eventual establishment of responsible government in the 1840s.

The 1837 rebellions were pivotal in shaping the future of the province, as they highlighted the growing desire for political change and the necessity of reform. By the time William Stewart was a teenager, many of the issues raised during the rebellions would begin to be addressed through political reform, and his life in Upper Canada would have been part of this evolving landscape.

AT 15 YEARS OLD IN 1848, William Stewart would have witnessed a significant political shift in Upper Canada with the establishment of the principle of responsible government.

The Responsible Government movement was a direct result of the 1837 Rebellions, where the people of Upper Canada, as well as Lower Canada, had demanded more control over their own political affairs, as opposed to being governed by appointed elites in Britain. The 1848 reforms granted the colonies more control over their own governance, allowing elected representatives to make decisions alongside the colonial executive. This marked the transition from a system where the governor had absolute power to one where the elected assembly held greater influence in decision-making.

For a 15-year-old like William, these changes would have been noticed, particularly in how the political environment was shifting. While William might not have fully understood the intricacies of responsible government, it would have been clear that the colonial government was becoming more responsive to the people, granting greater political rights and autonomy. It was a time of optimism for many in Upper Canada as they saw the beginning of a more democratic and locally-controlled system.

The establishment of responsible government meant that Upper Canada (and later, Ontario) would slowly begin to shed its more autocratic structures and become a part of a more balanced system, which would grow to shape Canada's future political landscape. For William, this was a time of growing political awareness, as this shift would influence both his own life and the broader society in which he lived.

IN 1861, AT 28 YEARS old, William Stewart would have been living in a rapidly changing society. As a farmer in Storrington, Ontario, William would have likely been engaged in agricultural work, which was the backbone of the economy during this time.

Given his Anglican faith, he would have been part of a community that was often closely knit around the church, which played a significant role in both social and spiritual life in rural Ontario. The Anglican Church would have been a focal point for social gatherings, as well as a place for worship and education.

The 1860s were a period of gradual progress in Ontario, with the construction of railways beginning to connect communities more efficiently, making it easier to ship goods and receive supplies. For a farmer like William, this shift would bring opportunities to expand trade and improve agricultural techniques. However, Ontario still had a rural, agrarian society, and farmers like William faced challenges such as maintaining their land, managing livestock, and dealing with the unpredictable nature of farming.

At 28, William might also have been considering his future—whether in terms of furthering his family, buying land, or seeking new opportunities in a growing province. The 1860s were a time of increasing immigration, economic development, and social change, all of which would shape William's outlook on life. The principle of responsible government introduced in 1848, which William had experienced in his youth, would have been settling into the fabric of Ontario's political identity. Ontario was gradually moving towards confederation, which would occur in 1867, and William, as a young adult, would have been aware of the political discussions shaping the future of Canada.

As a single man, William may have also been part of the growing social changes of the time, where new community events, technological advances, and social norms were influencing personal lives.

GENEALOGY ITINERARY:

Day 1: Arrival in Ontario

- Destination: Kingston, Ontario

- Activities:

- Check into a local hotel or bed and breakfast.

- Visit the Kingston Historical Society to gather preliminary information and resources about the region during the mid-19th century.

Day 2: Exploring Storrington

- Destination: Storrington, Ontario

- Activities:

- Visit the local archives or library to search for records related to William Stewart and his farming activities.

- Explore the area to get a sense of the landscape and environment where William lived and worked.

- Visit local Anglican churches to inquire about historical records and possibly view the church where William might have worshipped.

Day 3: Historical Research and Records

- Destination: Storrington, Ontario

- Activities:

- Spend the day at the local archives or library, focusing on census records, land records, and any other documents that might provide insights into William's life as a farmer.

- Meet with local historians or genealogy groups to discuss your findings and get additional leads.

Day 4: Visiting Cemeteries and Historical Sites

- Destination: Storrington, Ontario

- Activities:

- Visit local cemeteries to find gravesites of William Stewart and his family members.

- Explore historical sites and landmarks in the area to understand the context of William's life in the 1860s.

Day 5: Day Trip to Nearby Historical Locations

- Destination: Surrounding areas of Storrington

- Activities:

- Take a day trip to nearby towns and villages to explore additional archives, libraries, and historical societies.

- Visit any relevant museums or heritage sites that provide a broader understanding of life in Upper Canada during the 19th century.

Day 6: Reflection and Documentation

- Destination: Kingston, Ontario

- Activities:

- Return to Kingston to compile and document your findings.

- Visit the Kingston Frontenac Public Library for any final research and to use their genealogy resources.

- Reflect on the journey and prepare a summary of your discoveries to share with family members.

Day 7: Departure

- Destination: Home

- Activities:

- Check out of your accommodation and travel back home.

- Plan a family gathering to share the stories and information you uncovered about William Stewart.

MARTHA (UNKNOWN) STEWART

M ARTHA (UNKNOWN) STEWART[17]

Martha Stewart was born in 1788 in Ireland, during a period of great change for both her homeland and the world at large. Ireland, in the late 18th century, was under British rule, and the effects of the Irish Rebellion of 1798—an unsuccessful attempt for Irish independence—were still being felt across the country. The Act of Union in 1801 had unified Ireland with Great Britain, creating the United Kingdom of Great Britain and Ireland. These were turbulent times for the Irish, marked by political and social unrest.

Martha's early life would have likely been shaped by these political tensions. Depending on where she lived in Ireland, she may have witnessed or experienced the effects of these rebellions, or even been part of the growing tensions between the Catholic majority and Protestant elite. The Irish economy during this time was largely agrarian, and many families lived off the land, so Martha would have grown up in a rural environment, possibly involved in agriculture.

In 1815, when Martha would have been about 27 years old, the Irish famine began, which would later lead to large waves of emigration. By the time she was in her 30s, Ireland had been seeing more people leaving, particularly to places like North America.

Martha's life in Upper Canada (now Ontario) would have been shaped by this migration trend. If she emigrated in the early 19th century, her journey would have been part of the broader wave of Irish immigrants, many of whom settled in Ontario in the 1820s and 1830s. These immigrants brought with them Irish customs, language, and, in many cases, a desire for better opportunities and a new life away from the hardships of Ireland.

In 1861, when Martha would have been 73 years old, she would likely have been settled in Ontario, likely a part of the burgeoning agricultural community in Storrington. At this time, Ontario was a British colony, experiencing a period of growth and change. The social landscape was largely Anglican or Presbyterian, reflecting the religious makeup of the early settlers, and it is possible that Martha, being from Ireland, continued to practice the faith she brought with her from her homeland.

As an older woman in a rural community, Martha would likely have experienced the shift in generations and the evolving dynamics of her community, whether in terms of agriculture, religion, or social connections. She may have had children and grandchildren by 1861, helping to shape the future generations of the family. In Storrington, a small but growing community, Martha's life would have intertwined with the lives of other Irish immigrants, many of whom had similar stories of emigration, settlement, and building a new life in Upper Canada.

BY 1861, AT THE AGE of 73, Martha Stewart was living as a widow in Storrington, Ontario, and was Anglican in faith. Her life, having spanned several decades of significant social, political, and economic changes, would have reflected the challenges and adaptations that many immigrants, particularly Irish women, faced upon settling in a new land.

As a widow, Martha would have likely found her life increasingly shaped by her responsibilities to her family—whether that meant managing household duties or providing guidance to any children or grandchildren who might have been living with her. Given that the Anglican faith was prominent among many early settlers in the region, her religious identity would have been an integral part of her daily life. The Anglican community in Storrington would have provided her with both spiritual comfort and social support, with church services and community events likely being important gatherings in her life.

Storrington, which was part of Frontenac County in the eastern part of Ontario, would have been a rural community at the time, with a population made up largely of settlers from places like Ireland, Scotland, and England. The area would have been shaped by agriculture, and many residents were farmers or involved in related trades. While life in 1861 Ontario would have been more settled than when she first arrived as a young immigrant, Martha's days would have still been influenced by the rhythms of the seasons, the demands of her household, and her connection to the Anglican Church.

As a widow, Martha might have found strength in her faith and community ties, which would have provided her with emotional and practical support. The church would have been not just a place of worship but a central institution in her life. Storrington, though small, would have had a close-knit community of individuals who supported one another through both religious and social events.

Martha, having lived through the Irish Famine and emigrated to Upper Canada, would have been well aware of the immigrant experience, and she likely took part in community life alongside other Irish families, perhaps finding common ground with others who shared similar experiences. Her life would have been a testament to perseverance, as she navigated the difficulties of widowhood, raising children, and the complex realities of immigrant life in a changing colony.

GENEALOGY ITINERARY:

Day 1: Arrival in Ontario

- Destination: Kingston, Ontario

- Activities:

- Check into a local hotel or bed and breakfast.

- Visit the Kingston Historical Society to gather preliminary information and resources about the region during the mid-19th century.

Day 2: Exploring Storrington

- Destination: Storrington, Ontario

- Activities:

- Visit the local archives or library to search for records related to Martha Stewart and her family.

- Explore the area to get a sense of the landscape and environment where Martha lived.

- Visit local Anglican churches to inquire about historical records and possibly view the church where Martha might have worshipped.

Day 3: Historical Research and Records

- Destination: Storrington, Ontario

- Activities:

- Spend the day at the local archives or library, focusing on census records, land records, and any other documents that might provide insights into Martha's life.

- Meet with local historians or genealogy groups to discuss your findings and get additional leads.

Day 4: Visiting Cemeteries and Historical Sites

- Destination: Storrington, Ontario

- Activities:

- Visit local cemeteries to find gravesites of Martha Stewart and her family members.

- Explore historical sites and landmarks in the area to understand the context of Martha's life in the 1860s.

Day 5: Day Trip to Nearby Historical Locations

- Destination: Surrounding areas of Storrington

- Activities:

- Take a day trip to nearby towns and villages to explore additional archives, libraries, and historical societies.

- Visit any relevant museums or heritage sites that provide a broader understanding of life in Canada West during the 19th century.

Day 6: Reflection and Documentation

- Destination: Kingston, Ontario

- Activities:

- Return to Kingston to compile and document your findings.

- Visit the Kingston Frontenac Public Library for any final research and to use their genealogy resources.

- Reflect on the journey and prepare a summary of your discoveries to share with family members.

Day 7: Departure

- Destination: Home

- Activities:

- Check out of your accommodation and travel back home.

- Plan a family gathering to share the stories and information you uncovered about Martha Stewart.

PEETER STEWART

P EETER STEWART[18]

Peeter Stewart was born in Ireland in 1806. His early life would have been shaped by the political and social conditions of Ireland during the early 19th century, a time of great turmoil and change. The Act of Union in 1801 had united Ireland with Great Britain, creating the United Kingdom of Great Britain and Ireland. This period was marked by political unrest, particularly among the Irish population, who struggled with issues such as lack of representation, poverty, and discrimination.

As Peeter grew, he would have witnessed the effects of the Irish Rebellions and the ongoing tensions between the Irish people and the British government. The early 1800s were difficult years for many Irish, especially those living in rural areas, as famine and economic hardship took hold.

Peter's early years would likely have been influenced by these harsh realities. It's possible he was raised in a farming or working-class family, as many Irish people lived in these circumstances during this time.

If Peeter later immigrated to Canada—a common route for many Irish during the 19th century—he would have been one of the many Irish immigrants who fled Ireland's political and economic struggles. During the early to mid-1800s, Ireland faced a series of hardships, including the devastating Irish Famine (1845-1852). In the decades following the famine, a large wave of Irish immigrants made their way to Canada, seeking better opportunities.

As an immigrant, Peeter would have been part of the larger Irish community in Upper Canada (now Ontario), which was being shaped by these influxes of newcomers. Many Irish immigrants who arrived during this time settled in the rural parts of Ontario, such as Storrington, where agriculture and hard work defined much of daily life.

Peeter's later years would have been part of a new chapter in his life, likely marked by adjusting to life in Canada, finding community, and possibly starting a family. His experience as an Irish immigrant would have tied him to the larger historical story of Irish settlement in Canada.

IN 1861, PEETER STEWART was single, Anglican, and a farmer living in Storrington, Ontario. By this time, the region had seen a large influx of Irish settlers, and Peeter would have been part of this growing community of Irish immigrants.

As a farmer in Storrington, he would likely have been involved in the agricultural practices of the area, which were foundational to the economy of rural Ontario during this period. Life as a farmer was often hard work, but it provided opportunities for stability and land ownership, which were significant draws for immigrants from Ireland, many of whom were fleeing poverty and landlessness back home.

Being Anglican, Peeter would have been part of a faith community that played a central role in social life in Ontario at the time. Anglican churches served as both spiritual centers and community gathering points, offering a sense of belonging and connection to a larger network, especially for immigrants who were trying to build new lives in a foreign land.

As a single man, Peeter may have been focused on establishing himself in his new life, working the land, and possibly hoping to start a family in the future. The mid-19th century in Canada was a time of growth and change, especially in rural areas, where the economy was largely agrarian. Peeter's role as a farmer would have been integral to the development of the Storrington area as more settlers made their homes in the region.

Given his age, Peeter might have been in his early 50s by 1861, and though single, he could have had extended family or neighbors with whom he was close, as communities were often tightly knit, particularly among immigrant populations. Storrington was a rural and somewhat remote area, so social and religious life likely revolved around the local Anglican church, which would have provided a sense of community in an otherwise isolated environment.

GENEALOGY ITINERARY:

Day 1: Arrival in Ontario

- Destination: Kingston, Ontario

- Activities:

- Check into a local hotel or bed and breakfast.

- Visit the Kingston Historical Society to gather preliminary information and resources about the region during the mid-19th century.

Day 2: Exploring Storrington

- Destination: Storrington, Ontario

- Activities:

- Visit the local archives or library to search for records related to Peeter Stewart and his farming activities.

- Explore the area to get a sense of the landscape and environment where Peeter lived and worked.

- Visit local Anglican churches to inquire about historical records and possibly view the church where Peeter might have worshipped.

Day 3: Historical Research and Records

- Destination: Storrington, Ontario

- Activities:

- Spend the day at the local archives or library, focusing on census records, land records, and any other documents that might provide insights into Peeter's life as a farmer.

- Meet with local historians or genealogy groups to discuss your findings and get additional leads.

Day 4: Visiting Cemeteries and Historical Sites

- Destination: Storrington, Ontario

- Activities:

- Visit local cemeteries to find gravesites of Peeter Stewart and his family members.

- Explore historical sites and landmarks in the area to understand the context of Peeter's life in the 1860s.

Day 5: Day Trip to Nearby Historical Locations

- Destination: Surrounding areas of Storrington

- Activities:

- Take a day trip to nearby towns and villages to explore additional archives, libraries, and historical societies.

- Visit any relevant museums or heritage sites that provide a broader understanding of life in Canada West during the 19th century.

Day 6: Reflection and Documentation

- Destination: Kingston, Ontario

- Activities:

- Return to Kingston to compile and document your findings.

- Visit the Kingston Frontenac Public Library for any final research and to use their genealogy resources.

- Reflect on the journey and prepare a summary of your discoveries to share with family members.

Day 7: Departure

- Destination: Home

- Activities:

- Check out of your accommodation and travel back home.

- Plan a family gathering to share the stories and information you uncovered about Peeter Stewart.

REBECCA STEWART

REBECCA STEWART[19]

Rebecca Stewart was born in Canada West in 1844, during a time of significant change and development in the region. Canada West, which would later become Ontario following Confederation in 1867, was experiencing growing settlement, agricultural expansion, and increasing economic development.

Rebecca's birth came just a few years after the 1837-1838 Rebellions in Upper Canada, which had been a period of unrest and resistance against colonial authorities. By the time Rebecca was born, Canada West was beginning to stabilize under the leadership of the new Family Compact and Château Clique, which were replaced by new political movements pushing for more democratic governance.

In 1844, Canada West had a predominantly agricultural economy, and many immigrants, particularly from Ireland and Britain, were settling in the region, establishing farms and communities. Rebecca, born in this time, would have likely been part of a growing immigrant population, as many of her contemporaries were descendants of Irish, British, and other European settlers.

By the time she reached adulthood, Rebecca would have experienced the expansion of the railway system and increasing economic opportunities in the region, as well as the growing tension between the English-speaking Protestant settlers and the French-speaking Catholic communities in the province. These dynamics would shape much of her life and that of her community. In 1861, at age 17, Rebecca would be living in a Canada that was on the cusp of significant political change and moving toward the eventual Confederation in 1867.

IN 1861, REBECCA STEWART would have been 17 years old and living in Storrington, Ontario, a rural township in Frontenac County. At this time, Storrington was a predominantly agricultural area, and life was centered around farming, community life, and religious practices.

As an Anglican in a small rural community, Rebecca's religious life would have been important, with the Anglican Church playing a central role in social gatherings, holidays, and rites of passage such as baptisms, marriages, and funerals. The Anglican Church had a significant presence in Ontario during this period, and it provided spiritual guidance and a sense of community for many.

At 17, Rebecca would have likely been finishing her formal education, which for most children in rural Ontario at the time would have been limited to basic reading, writing, and arithmetic, often through a one-room schoolhouse. Much of her education would have also come from family, church, and community experiences, including learning domestic skills, farming techniques, and social norms.

In Storrington, life would have been influenced by the seasons, with farming at the core of daily life. Depending on her family's occupation, Rebecca may have helped with farm work, caring for livestock, tending to crops, and participating in household chores.

1861 was a time of political and social change in Ontario. The Province of Canada was experiencing increasing calls for responsible government, which would be achieved in 1867 with Confederation. This time of reform and change, particularly the expansion of transportation and infrastructure like the railroads, brought new opportunities and challenges to rural communities like Storrington.

At 17, Rebecca may have been starting to think about her future, including the possibility of marriage and starting a family, both of which were common life milestones for women of her time. It was also the beginning of an era where many young women began to have more control over their own lives as the role of women in society started to evolve with the changing times.

Her life in Storrington would have been deeply intertwined with her family and local community, and the landscape of Ontario's agricultural society would shape much of her daily existence.

GENEALOGY ITINERARY:

DAY 1: ARRIVAL IN ONTARIO

- Destination: Kingston, Ontario

- Activities:

- Check into a local hotel or bed and breakfast.

- Visit the Kingston Historical Society to gather preliminary information and resources about the region during the mid-19th century.

Day 2: Exploring Storrington

- Destination: Storrington, Ontario

- Activities:

- Visit the local archives or library to search for records related to Rebecca Stewart and her family.

- Explore the area to get a sense of the landscape and environment where Rebecca lived.

- Visit local Presbyterian and Anglican churches to inquire about historical records and possibly view the churches where Rebecca might have worshipped.

Day 3: Historical Research and Records

- Destination: Storrington, Ontario

- Activities:

- Spend the day at the local archives or library, focusing on census records, land records, and any other documents that might provide insights into Rebecca's life.

- Meet with local historians or genealogy groups to discuss your findings and get additional leads.

Day 4: Visiting Cemeteries and Historical Sites

- Destination: Storrington, Ontario

- Activities:

- Visit local cemeteries to find gravesites of Rebecca Stewart and her family members.

- Explore historical sites and landmarks in the area to understand the context of Rebecca's life in the 1860s.

Day 5: Day Trip to Nearby Historical Locations

- Destination: Surrounding areas of Storrington

- Activities:

- Take a day trip to nearby towns and villages to explore additional archives, libraries, and historical societies.

- Visit any relevant museums or heritage sites that provide a broader understanding of life in Canada West during the 19th century.

Day 6: Reflection and Documentation

- Destination: Kingston, Ontario

- Activities:

- Return to Kingston to compile and document your findings.

- Visit the Kingston Frontenac Public Library for any final research and to use their genealogy resources.

- Reflect on the journey and prepare a summary of your discoveries to share with family members.

Day 7: Departure

- Destination: Home

- Activities:

- Check out of your accommodation and travel back home.

- Plan a family gathering to share the stories and information you uncovered about Rebecca Stewart.

ALEX McWATTERS

A LEX McWATTERS[20]

Alex McWatters, born in Upper Canada in 1831, grew up during a transformative time in Canadian history. Upper Canada (now Ontario) was a British colony experiencing growth and change, particularly as settlers expanded agriculture, built communities, and established trade.

In his early years, Alex would have witnessed the following:

Agricultural Society: Life in rural Upper Canada revolved around farming. Settlers like Alex's family likely engaged in subsistence farming, growing crops like wheat, barley, and potatoes, and raising livestock for their survival and trade.

Transportation: The Rideau Canal, completed in 1832, would have enhanced transportation and trade near some settlements, promoting economic growth and connecting rural areas to larger markets.

Education and Religion: Access to education was limited but expanding through local efforts. Religion played a central role in family and community life, with many settlers adhering to Anglican, Presbyterian, or Methodist denominations.

Political Context: In 1837, when Alex was six, the Rebellions of Upper and Lower Canada occurred. These uprisings sought political reform and responsible government. Although Alex would have been too young to remember details, the rebellions likely influenced conversations in his community.

Population Growth: Immigration from Ireland, Scotland, and England continued to shape Upper Canada's demographics, especially after the Irish famine of the 1840s.

BY 1861, ALEX MCWATTERS was 30 years old, married, Presbyterian, and working as a farmer in Upper Canada (by then known as Canada West). His life would have revolved around the rhythms of agricultural work, family responsibilities, and church involvement.

Daily Life in 1861

Farming: As a farmer, Alex likely managed crops such as wheat, oats, and potatoes, alongside livestock like cows, pigs, and chickens. Farming was labor-intensive, relying on family members and occasionally neighbors for help during harvest seasons.

Community and Church: Being Presbyterian, Alex would have been active in his church, which was a cornerstone of both spiritual life and social interaction in rural areas. Sunday services and church events provided opportunities to connect with neighbors and discuss community matters.

Family Life: Marriage brought added responsibilities, as Alex and his wife would have worked together to maintain their home, raise children (if they had any by then), and manage the farm. His wife would have been responsible for household chores, gardening, and possibly assisting with farm work.

BROADER CONTEXT IN 1861

Agricultural Development: By this time, farming in Canada West had advanced with the use of new tools like horse-drawn plows and reapers, increasing productivity.

Census of 1861: The year marked Canada's first detailed census, reflecting the growing population and the diversity of Upper Canada's settlers. Alex's household would have been included, listing details about his family, land, and livestock.

Railroads and Trade: The expanding railroad network in Canada West offered farmers like Alex better access to markets, enabling them to sell surplus produce and purchase goods more easily.

Presbyterian Church Growth: The Presbyterian community was strong, reflecting the influence of Scottish settlers in Canada West. The church also played a significant role in education and local governance.

ALEX'S LIFE IN 1861 would have been shaped by hard work, a strong connection to his faith, and the gradual modernization of farming practices in a developing rural society.

GENEALOGY ITINERARY:

Day 1: Arrival in Ontario

- Destination: Kingston, Ontario

- Activities:

- Check into a local hotel or bed and breakfast.

- Visit the Kingston Historical Society to gather preliminary information and resources about the region during the mid-19th century.

Day 2: Exploring Storrington

• Destination: Storrington, Ontario

• Activities:

• Visit the local archives or library to search for records related to Alex McWatters and his farming activities.

• Explore the area to get a sense of the landscape and environment where Alex lived and worked.

• Visit local Presbyterian churches to inquire about historical records and possibly view the church where Alex and his family might have worshipped.

Day 3: Historical Research and Records

• Destination: Storrington, Ontario

• Activities:

• Spend the day at the local archives or library, focusing on census records, land records, and any other documents that might provide insights into Alex's life as a farmer.

• Meet with local historians or genealogy groups to discuss your findings and get additional leads.

Day 4: Visiting Cemeteries and Historical Sites

• Destination: Storrington, Ontario

• Activities:

• Visit local cemeteries to find gravesites of Alex McWatters and his family members.

- Explore historical sites and landmarks in the area to understand the context of Alex's life in the 1860s.

Day 5: Day Trip to Nearby Historical Locations

- Destination: Surrounding areas of Storrington

- Activities:

- Take a day trip to nearby towns and villages to explore additional archives, libraries, and historical societies.

- Visit any relevant museums or heritage sites that provide a broader understanding of life in Upper Canada during the 19th century.

Day 6: Reflection and Documentation

- Destination: Kingston, Ontario

- Activities:

- Return to Kingston to compile and document your findings.

- Visit the Kingston Frontenac Public Library for any final research and to use their genealogy resources.

- Reflect on the journey and prepare a summary of your discoveries to share with family members.

Day 7: Departure

- Destination: Home

- Activities:

- Check out of your accommodation and travel back home.

- Plan a family gathering to share the stories and information you uncovered about Alex McWatters.

MARGARET (UNKNOWN) McWATTERS

MARGARET (UNKNOWN) McWATTERS[21]

Life in Ireland in 1833 was defined by a mix of agrarian traditions, political unrest, and economic challenges. Margaret McWatters' early years would have been shaped by the following:

Economic Context

Agriculture-Based Economy: Most Irish families relied on subsistence farming, with the potato as the staple crop. Land was often rented from absentee landlords, and tenant farmers lived under the threat of eviction if rents were not paid.

Poverty and Inequality: The rural population faced widespread poverty. Land was divided into smaller plots to support growing families, exacerbating economic difficulties.

SOCIAL AND CULTURAL Life

Strong Community Bonds: Irish society was deeply rooted in local communities. Church and family played central roles, offering support and stability amid hardships.

Oral Traditions and Music: Margaret's childhood may have been filled with traditional Irish songs, storytelling, and cultural practices passed down through generations.

RELIGION

Religious Divide: Tensions between Catholics and Protestants were significant. By 1833, political reforms such as Catholic Emancipation (1829) allowed Catholics to enter public life, but sectarian divides persisted.

POLITICAL CLIMATE

Reform Movements: The period saw increasing calls for tenant rights, political representation, and independence from British rule. Daniel O'Connell's campaign for Catholic rights was a major influence at the time.

DAILY LIFE

Living Conditions: Rural homes were often small, with thatched roofs and earthen floors. Families lived modestly, with limited access to education or healthcare.

Work and Roles: Women like Margaret would have helped with farm work, cared for younger siblings, and contributed to household chores from an early age.

GLOBAL CONTEXT

Industrial Revolution: While Ireland remained agrarian, industrial advances in Britain were beginning to influence Ireland's cities, leading to urban migration for those seeking work.

MARGARET WAS BORN INTO an Ireland on the cusp of change, where traditions and hardships coexisted. Her early experiences likely instilled resilience, resourcefulness, and a deep connection to her Irish heritage, traits she carried with her to Upper Canada.

MARGARET MCWATTERS was six years old in 1839 when the Irish Hurricane struck. This catastrophic storm, one of the most severe to hit Ireland, would have left a significant impression on her early childhood.

Impact of the Irish Hurricane (1839):

Widespread Destruction: The hurricane, known as "The Night of the Big Wind," tore through Ireland on January 6–7, 1839, destroying homes, farms, and infrastructure. Entire villages were flattened, and roofs were ripped off houses, leaving families exposed to the elements.

Loss of Life: Though exact figures are unknown, there were numerous fatalities. Margaret may have witnessed or heard of the devastation affecting her community.

Economic Hardship: Already impoverished farmers lost crops, livestock, and livelihoods, deepening the poverty many Irish families endured.

Childhood Memories: For a child like Margaret, the event would have been terrifying—howling winds, darkness, and the chaos of adults attempting to protect their homes and families.

THIS STORM WAS SO IMPACTFUL that it became a cultural marker in Irish history, and it would have been a shared memory among Margaret's generation.

MARGARET MCWATTERS was 12 years old in 1845 when the Irish Immigration began due to the Great Famine. This event marked a pivotal moment in Irish history, and as a young girl, Margaret would have been deeply affected by the societal upheaval.

The Great Famine and Irish Immigration (1845):

The Potato Blight: In 1845, a devastating potato blight struck Ireland, destroying the primary food source for millions of Irish people, particularly the rural poor.

Mass Starvation and Disease: The famine led to widespread starvation, disease, and desperation. Families were often forced to sell or abandon everything to survive or seek a better life elsewhere.

Emigration Waves: Many Irish families fled to places like Canada, the United States, and Australia. The journey was grueling, with overcrowded ships (nicknamed "coffin ships") leading to high mortality rates.

MARGARET'S PERSPECTIVE at Age 12:

Witnessing Hardship: Margaret may have seen friends or relatives emigrate, leaving behind a land rife with suffering and uncertainty. If her family remained in Ireland during this time, they likely experienced severe food shortages, economic strain, and the emotional toll of seeing their community fractured.

Connection to Canada: By 1861, Margaret lived in Storrington, Ontario, suggesting her family might have emigrated as part of this wave or shortly after. Like many others, they may have sought refuge and opportunity in the Canadian colonies.

MARGARET'S CHILDHOOD in famine-era Ireland would have shaped her resilience and perspective as she built a new life in Canada.

IN 1861, MARGARET MCWATTERS, aged 28, was living in Storrington, Ontario, and identified as Presbyterian. Having emigrated from Ireland, she likely carried memories of the Great Famine and the Irish immigration wave of 1845.

Margaret's Life in 1861:

Community and Faith: As a Presbyterian in Storrington, she was part of a strong Protestant community. Churches often provided not only spiritual guidance but also a social hub for immigrants adjusting to life in Upper Canada.

Rural Life: Storrington was a farming community, so Margaret's daily life would have revolved around agricultural work, household duties, and community events.

Cultural Adaptation: She was likely adapting to a new identity as a Canadian while maintaining Irish traditions. The famine and her journey to Canada may have made her especially resourceful and focused on building a stable life.

MARGARET'S RESILIENCE and faith would have been central to her experience as an immigrant carving out a new life in Canada West.

GENEALOGY ITINERARY:

Day 1: Arrival in Ontario

- Destination: Kingston, Ontario

- Activities:

- Check into a local hotel or bed and breakfast.

- Visit the Kingston Historical Society to gather preliminary information and resources about the region during the mid-19th century.

Day 2: Exploring Storrington

- Destination: Storrington, Ontario

- Activities:

- Visit the local archives or library to search for records related to Margaret McWatters and her family.

- Explore the area to get a sense of the landscape and environment where Margaret lived.

- Visit local Presbyterian churches to inquire about historical records and possibly view the church where Margaret and her family might have worshipped.

Day 3: Historical Research and Records

- Destination: Storrington, Ontario

- Activities:

- Spend the day at the local archives or library, focusing on census records, land records, and any other documents that might provide insights into Margaret's life as a farmer's wife.

- Meet with local historians or genealogy groups to discuss your findings and get additional leads.

Day 4: Visiting Cemeteries and Historical Sites

- Destination: Storrington, Ontario

- Activities:

- Visit local cemeteries to find gravesites of Margaret McWatters and her family members.

- Explore historical sites and landmarks in the area to understand the context of Margaret's life in the 1860s.

Day 5: Day Trip to Nearby Historical Locations

- Destination: Surrounding areas of Storrington

- Activities:

- Take a day trip to nearby towns and villages to explore additional archives, libraries, and historical societies.

- Visit any relevant museums or heritage sites that provide a broader understanding of life in Canada West during the 19th century.

Day 6: Reflection and Documentation

- Destination: Kingston, Ontario

- Activities:

- Return to Kingston to compile and document your findings.

- Visit the Kingston Frontenac Public Library for any final research and to use their genealogy resources.

- Reflect on the journey and prepare a summary of your discoveries to share with family members.

Day 7: Departure

- Destination: Home

- Activities:

- Check out of your accommodation and travel back home.

- Plan a family gathering to share the stories and information you uncovered about Margaret McWatters.

MARGARET McWATTERS

MARGARET McWATTERS[22]

Margaret McWatters, the daughter of Alex and Margaret McWatters, was born in Canada West in 1858. Her early childhood was shaped by the rural and agricultural lifestyle of Storrington, Ontario, where her family lived.

Life in 1858:

Canada West in Transition: The colony was experiencing economic growth and social change. Railways were expanding, connecting towns and fostering trade. However, rural areas like Storrington remained primarily farming communities, where daily life revolved around agricultural work.

Immigrant Influence: As the child of Irish immigrants, young Margaret grew up in a household that likely blended Irish traditions with the emerging Canadian identity.

Family Faith: As Presbyterians, her family's religious practices would have been central to their routine, shaping her upbringing and community interactions.

BY THE TIME MARGARET turned 3 in 1861, she was living with her parents in Storrington, part of a hardworking farming family connected to a larger network of Irish immigrants in Ontario.

GENEALOGY ITINERARY:

Day 1: Arrival in Ontario

- Destination: Kingston, Ontario

- Activities:

- Check into a local hotel or bed and breakfast.

- Visit the Kingston Historical Society to gather preliminary information and resources about the region during the mid-19th century.

Day 2: Exploring Storrington

- Destination: Storrington, Ontario

- Activities:

- Visit the local archives or library to search for records related to Margaret McWatters and her family.

- Explore the area to get a sense of the landscape and environment where Margaret lived.

- Visit local Presbyterian churches to inquire about historical records and possibly view the church where Margaret and her family might have worshipped.

Day 3: Historical Research and Records

- Destination: Storrington, Ontario

- Activities:

- Spend the day at the local archives or library, focusing on census records, land records, and any other documents that might provide insights into Margaret's life as a farmer's daughter.

- Meet with local historians or genealogy groups to discuss your findings and get additional leads.

Day 4: Visiting Cemeteries and Historical Sites

- Destination: Storrington, Ontario

- Activities:

- Visit local cemeteries to find gravesites of Margaret McWatters and her family members.

- Explore historical sites and landmarks in the area to understand the context of Margaret's life in the 1860s.

Day 5: Day Trip to Nearby Historical Locations

- Destination: Surrounding areas of Storrington

- Activities:

- Take a day trip to nearby towns and villages to explore additional archives, libraries, and historical societies.

- Visit any relevant museums or heritage sites that provide a broader understanding of life in Canada West during the 19th century.

Day 6: Reflection and Documentation

- Destination: Kingston, Ontario

- Activities:

- Return to Kingston to compile and document your findings.

- Visit the Kingston Frontenac Public Library for any final research and to use their genealogy resources.

- Reflect on the journey and prepare a summary of your discoveries to share with family members.

Day 7: Departure

- Destination: Home

- Activities:

- Check out of your accommodation and travel back home.

- Plan a family gathering to share the stories and information you uncovered about Margaret McWatters.

CATHRINE McWATTERS

CATHRINE McWATTERS[23]

Cathrine McWatters, the daughter of Alex and Margaret McWatters, was born in Canada West in 1860. Her infancy coincided with a period of development and change in Ontario as it moved closer to Confederation.

Life in 1860:

Canada West (Ontario): Rural areas like Storrington were primarily agricultural, with families relying on farming for sustenance and trade. The population was growing steadily, and small communities were the backbone of Canadian society.

Family Life: As the youngest child, Cathrine would have grown up in a close-knit family with her older sister, Margaret. Her parents' Irish heritage and Presbyterian faith would have been strong influences in her early upbringing.

Local Connections: The McWatters family likely participated in their local Presbyterian church, which would have been a hub for social and religious activities in the community.

BY 1861, CATHRINE WAS just a baby, living with her family in Storrington, Ontario, surrounded by the natural beauty and challenges of pioneer life in Canada West.

GENEALOGY ITINERARY:

Day 1: Arrival in Ontario

• Destination: Kingston, Ontario

• Activities:

• Check into a local hotel or bed and breakfast.

• Visit the Kingston Historical Society to gather preliminary information and resources about the region during the mid-19th century.

Day 2: Exploring Storrington

• Destination: Storrington, Ontario

• Activities:

• Visit the local archives or library to search for records related to Cathrine McWatters and her family.

• Explore the area to get a sense of the landscape and environment where Cathrine lived.

• Visit local Presbyterian churches to inquire about historical records and possibly view the church where Cathrine and her family might have worshipped.

Day 3: Historical Research and Records

• Destination: Storrington, Ontario

• Activities:

• Spend the day at the local archives or library, focusing on census records, land records, and any other documents that might provide insights into Cathrine's life as a farmer's daughter.

- Meet with local historians or genealogy groups to discuss your findings and get additional leads.

Day 4: Visiting Cemeteries and Historical Sites

- Destination: Storrington, Ontario
- Activities:
- Visit local cemeteries to find gravesites of Cathrine McWatters and her family members.
- Explore historical sites and landmarks in the area to understand the context of Cathrine's life in the 1860s.

Day 5: Day Trip to Nearby Historical Locations

- Destination: Surrounding areas of Storrington
- Activities:
- Take a day trip to nearby towns and villages to explore additional archives, libraries, and historical societies.
- Visit any relevant museums or heritage sites that provide a broader understanding of life in Canada West during the 19th century.

Day 6: Reflection and Documentation

- Destination: Kingston, Ontario
- Activities:
- Return to Kingston to compile and document your findings.
- Visit the Kingston Frontenac Public Library for any final research and to use their genealogy resources.

- Reflect on the journey and prepare a summary of your discoveries to share with family members.

Day 7: Departure

- Destination: Home

- Activities:

- Check out of your accommodation and travel back home.

- Plan a family gathering to share the stories and information you uncovered about Cathrine McWatters.

JOHN McWATTERS

JOHN McWATTERS[24]

John McWaters' birth in Ireland in 1791 took place during a tumultuous time in Irish history, marked by both political upheaval and significant cultural shifts. Here's an overview of life in Ireland during this period:

Political and Social Context:

British Rule: Ireland was under British control, with the Protestant Ascendancy dominating politics and land ownership. Catholics, who made up the majority of the population, faced severe restrictions under the Penal Laws, limiting their rights to own land, vote, or hold public office.

United Irishmen Movement: In the 1790s, the Society of United Irishmen began organizing to advocate for Irish independence and greater equality among religious groups. This would eventually lead to the Irish Rebellion of 1798, a pivotal event in Irish history.

Economic Hardships: The rural Irish population was heavily reliant on agriculture, particularly the potato, which had become a staple crop. Many small tenant farmers lived in poverty, struggling under high rents and limited resources.

DAILY LIFE:

Rural Life: Most of the population lived in small villages or rural areas, farming potatoes, oats, and livestock. Houses were typically simple, made of stone or mud, with thatched roofs.

Family Structure: Large families were common, as children contributed to household labor. Education opportunities were limited, particularly for Catholics and the poor.

Clothing: Clothing was practical and made from wool or linen. Hand-spun and woven garments were the norm for most rural families.

Religion: Religious practices were central to life. Catholics often worshipped in secret or in makeshift churches due to restrictions, while the Anglican Church maintained official dominance.

BROADER HISTORICAL Events:

French Revolutionary Influence: The ideas of liberty and equality spreading from the French Revolution (1789–1799) influenced Irish movements, inspiring hope among reformers and fear among British authorities.

Industrial Revolution: While Ireland was primarily agrarian, the Industrial Revolution was beginning to transform parts of the country, particularly around Belfast.

JOHN MCWATERS WOULD have been born into a society shaped by inequality and struggle, with resilience and community playing significant roles in daily life. His experiences as an Irishman born during this era would reflect these broader historical currents.

AT AGE 16 IN 1807, John McWaters witnessed a groundbreaking advancement in transportation: the launch of Robert Fulton's Clermont, the first commercially successful steamboat. This invention revolutionized travel and trade by enabling faster and more reliable water transport.

Context in 1807:

Steamboats and Ireland: Although the Clermont operated in the United States, steamboat technology eventually impacted Ireland, particularly in coastal and river trade routes. Steam-powered vessels allowed for quicker transport of goods and passengers, influencing economic growth and migration patterns, including later Irish emigration to North America.

Global Changes: The Napoleonic Wars (1803–1815) dominated global affairs, and Ireland was deeply affected by its role within the British Empire. Trade disruptions and blockades influenced Irish ports and agriculture.

Local Life: For rural Irish communities, such technological advancements might have felt distant. However, innovations like steamboats represented progress and hinted at a world growing more interconnected, something that would later influence Irish emigration and industrial growth.

FOR SOMEONE LIKE JOHN, living in Ireland during this period, the invention of the steamboat would have seemed remarkable but still far removed from his daily life, which likely centered around farming and surviving under challenging social and economic conditions.

AT 35 YEARS OLD IN 1826, John McWaters lived during a time of small but significant technological advancements, one of which was the invention of friction matches by John Walker in England. These early matches, known as "lucifers," made it easier to produce fire, replacing more cumbersome methods like flint and steel.

Context in 1826:

Impact of Matches: While it took time for matches to become widely available and affordable, their invention eventually revolutionized daily life, simplifying tasks like lighting candles, lamps, and stoves. For rural communities in Ireland, this innovation made home and hearth more manageable, though it may not have been immediately accessible to all due to cost or distribution challenges.

Life in Ireland: The 1820s were a time of gradual change in Ireland, with ongoing social and economic struggles under British rule. Agricultural communities, like the one John likely came from, were heavily reliant on traditional methods of subsistence farming. Access to modern conveniences, even small ones like matches, could symbolize progress and hope for a better quality of life.

Broader World Events: The Industrial Revolution was well underway in Britain, and its effects were beginning to ripple through Ireland. Innovations like matches were part of a larger trend of new tools and technologies improving productivity and convenience.

FOR JOHN, THE INVENTION of matches may have been more of a distant curiosity initially, but over time, it would become an everyday item that simplified life in profound ways.

AT 48 YEARS OLD IN 1839, John McWaters would have experienced the Irish Hurricane of that year, a rare and powerful storm that struck Ireland in November 1839. The hurricane caused significant damage, particularly along the southwestern coast of Ireland, uprooting trees, destroying homes, and taking lives.

Context in 1839:

Irish Hurricane: The storm was one of the most intense tropical cyclones to impact Ireland in the 19th century. It caused widespread destruction, especially in coastal regions, with winds reaching as high as 100 mph. Many areas were left in disarray, and the damage affected the economy, especially in rural and farming communities.

John McWaters' Perspective: As a man in his late 40s, John would have lived through various hardships and witnessed the resilience of rural communities in Ireland. The hurricane would have been another harsh reminder of nature's power, but it also reinforced the necessity of preparation and the tight-knit nature of communities, especially in the face of such destructive events.

Impact on Daily Life: For someone like John, living through the hurricane could have meant rebuilding homes, securing the land, and helping neighbors recover from the storm. The hurricane's aftermath likely influenced farming practices, as agricultural lands may have been damaged, which could have disrupted the livelihoods of many families in his area.

IN THE BROADER CONTEXT of 1839, John's life was shaped by Ireland's economic difficulties, the struggle for independence, and the devastation of natural disasters, but it also marked an era of resilience and rebuilding. The Irish Hurricane would have been an event of significant local impact that John would have likely remembered as a moment of collective hardship and recovery.

IN 1845, WHEN JOHN McWaters was 54 years old, Ireland was facing a major crisis due to the Great Famine, which began that year. This led to a wave of Irish immigration, particularly in the years following 1845.

Context of 1845:

The Great Famine: The potato crop failure of 1845, caused by a potato blight, triggered the famine that would ravage Ireland for several years. With the potato being the staple food for much of the population, the crop failure led to widespread starvation and disease. The Irish government's inadequate response, combined with ongoing poverty and British colonial policies, made the situation even worse.

Impact on John McWaters: As a 54-year-old man, John would have seen the deepening misery and economic hardship caused by the famine. His personal experience would likely have been shaped by the economic collapse around him, as agricultural communities struggled with crop failures and increasing poverty. If John lived in a rural area, as many did during this time, he may have witnessed the devastation of farms and the immense pressure to survive.

Immigration: The famine drove millions of Irish people to emigrate, mostly to countries like Canada, the United States, and Australia. By 1845, John might have seen friends, relatives, and neighbors making the difficult decision to leave Ireland in search of food and better opportunities. The Irish immigration to places like Canada was part of a larger trend, and many Irish immigrants would have settled in Ontario, Quebec, and other regions.

For John, the rise in emigration could have been both a painful and a hopeful event. It would have marked the departure of loved ones, but also the possibility of new opportunities in the New World. If John was connected to any of the emigrants, he might have seen them off or heard their stories from those who returned. His own decision to stay in Ireland may have been influenced by family ties, his livelihood, or the hope of surviving the famine.

IN SUMMARY, 1845 WAS a pivotal year in Irish history, and for John McWaters, it was a time of personal reflection amid societal upheaval. The famine and subsequent immigration would have left a lasting impact on his life, either through the loss of family and friends or through witnessing the migration of his fellow countrymen.

IN 1861, JOHN MCWATERS would have been 70 years old, living in Storrington, Ontario, as a Presbyterian and a farmer.

Life in 1861 for John McWaters:

1. Age and Health: At 70, John would be considered quite elderly for the time. In the mid-19th century, the average life expectancy was much lower than it is today, so reaching 70 would have been an impressive milestone. However, age might have also brought challenges, such as declining health, particularly given the hard, manual work involved in farming. He may have relied more on his children or other family members for help on the farm, though many elderly people in rural areas remained active as long as possible.

---

2. PRESBYTERIAN FAITH: As a Presbyterian, John would likely have been a part of a close-knit religious community. Religion played a central role in the lives of many rural families, offering spiritual support and a sense of community. Sunday church services, prayer meetings, and religious festivals would have been an important part of his life. His faith, especially in the context of the hardships he may have experienced—such as surviving the Irish famine and possibly the migration to Canada—might have provided comfort and strength.

---

3. FARMING LIFE: AS a farmer, John would have been accustomed to the rhythms of rural life, marked by planting and harvest seasons, caring for animals, and maintaining the land. By 1861, farming in Storrington, Ontario would likely have been shaped by both traditional methods and some new innovations. The 1850s had seen technological advances, including the use of steel plows and the introduction of new farming tools that made the work somewhat more efficient, though it remained grueling. John might have also seen some changes in the market, with increased settlement in Ontario and new opportunities for farming, though land could still be difficult to work due to the dense forests in parts of Storrington.

---

4. COMMUNITY AND IMMIGRATION: By 1861, Storrington, located in what was then Canada West, was becoming more settled, with many families of Irish descent. As someone who had likely witnessed Irish immigration to Ontario, John would have been part of a community of immigrants who had come from Ireland during the famine years. Many of these Irish immigrants settled in rural areas, where they could farm the land. John may have been involved in local community affairs, including religious activities, helping newcomers, or providing mentorship to younger settlers. He would have seen the

evolution of the town as more families, particularly from Ireland and Scotland, arrived.

5. POLITICAL AND SOCIAL Climate: In 1861, Canada West was beginning to experience major political and social changes. The Province of Canada (which included Canada West and Canada East) was still under British control but was moving toward confederation. Discussions around responsible government and the desire for self-governance would have been central to local and national conversations. As someone who lived through some of the tumultuous history of Ireland, particularly the Irish Famine and its aftermath, John may have had a strong sense of political awareness and an opinion about these shifts, particularly with respect to how they might impact his life as an immigrant.

IN SUMMARY, 1861 WOULD have been a year of reflection for John McWaters as he aged, rooted in his Presbyterian faith and the rural, agricultural life in Storrington. It was a time when he would have witnessed the maturation of the community around him, the continued influence of Irish immigration, and the broader political changes in Canada West.

GENEALOGY ITINERARY:

DAY 1: ARRIVAL IN ONTARIO

- Destination: Kingston, Ontario
- Activities:

- Check into a local hotel or bed and breakfast.

- Visit the Kingston Historical Society to gather preliminary information and resources about the region during the mid-19th century.

Day 2: Exploring Storrington

- Destination: Storrington, Ontario

- Activities:

- Visit the local archives or library to search for records related to John McWatters and his farming activities.

- Explore the area to get a sense of the landscape and environment where John lived and worked.

- Visit local Presbyterian churches to inquire about historical records and possibly view the church where John and his family might have worshipped.

Day 3: Historical Research and Records

- Destination: Storrington, Ontario

- Activities:

- Spend the day at the local archives or library, focusing on census records, land records, and any other documents that might provide insights into John's life as a farmer.

- Meet with local historians or genealogy groups to discuss your findings and get additional leads.

Day 4: Visiting Cemeteries and Historical Sites

- Destination: Storrington, Ontario

- Activities:

- Visit local cemeteries to find gravesites of John McWatters and his family members.

- Explore historical sites and landmarks in the area to understand the context of John's life in the 1860s.

Day 5: Day Trip to Nearby Historical Locations

- Destination: Surrounding areas of Storrington

- Activities:

- Take a day trip to nearby towns and villages to explore additional archives, libraries, and historical societies.

- Visit any relevant museums or heritage sites that provide a broader understanding of life in Canada West during the 19th century.

Day 6: Reflection and Documentation

- Destination: Kingston, Ontario

- Activities:

- Return to Kingston to compile and document your findings.

- Visit the Kingston Frontenac Public Library for any final research and to use their genealogy resources.

- Reflect on the journey and prepare a summary of your discoveries to share with family members.

Day 7: Departure

- Destination: Home

- Activities:

- Check out of your accommodation and travel back home.

- Plan a family gathering to share the stories and information you uncovered about John McWatters.

CATHRINE McWATTERS

CATHRINE McWATTERS[25]

Cathrine McWatters was born in Ireland in 1801, during a period of significant change and upheaval in Irish history. Here's what life was likely like in Ireland and her early years up until the time she emigrated:

Life in Ireland Around 1801:

1. Political and Social Landscape:

Ireland in 1801 was under British rule, having formally joined the United Kingdom of Great Britain and Ireland through the Act of Union. This marked the dissolution of the Irish Parliament and the merging of Irish governance with Britain.

At the time, many Irish people were Catholic and faced significant religious discrimination by the Protestant ruling class. Tensions between the two groups were high, and there was significant unrest, including the Irish Rebellions that sought independence from British control.

The Act of Union caused political friction and created a sense of loss for many Irish nationalists, though it also solidified the control of the Protestant Ascendancy in Ireland.

2. DAILY LIFE:

The early 1800s were challenging for most rural Irish families, especially in the countryside. People lived primarily in small farmhouses, with subsistence farming being common. Families cultivated crops like potatoes, oats, and wheat, while livestock (primarily cattle, sheep, and pigs) were also raised.

Living conditions were often poor for the working class. Many Irish farmers were tenants, often struggling with landlords who could evict them at will. There were also frequent famine years, particularly in the 1830s, which led to crop failures and hunger for many rural Irish families.

---

3. EDUCATION AND OPPORTUNITIES:

Cathrine, depending on her family's wealth and background, may not have had much access to formal education, as education was a luxury for the wealthier classes, particularly for women. Most Irish children would have learned basic reading, writing, and arithmetic, if at all.

In this period, opportunities for women were limited. Cathrine would have been expected to learn domestic duties, including cooking, cleaning, and caring for the home and family. Marriage and motherhood were typically seen as the primary roles for women during this time.

---

4. EMIGRATION AND EARLY Life in Canada:

By the time Cathrine reached adulthood, Ireland was facing the 1800s agricultural crises and increasing poverty, leading many to seek opportunities elsewhere, particularly in North America. Cathrine may have been one of those Irish immigrants who left for better prospects, especially as conditions worsened leading up to the Irish Famine.

Cathrine's emigration might have occurred as part of the larger wave of Irish immigration to Canada that took place in the 1830s and 1840s. The prospect of cheap land in Canada West (modern-day Ontario) and the growing demand for labor in the New World may have been factors in her decision to migrate.

Life in Canada:

When Cathrine arrived in Canada, she would have found herself among a growing Irish immigrant community in the Ontario region, particularly as many Irish had settled in the Storrington area of Canada West (modern-day Ontario). Many Irish immigrants in the region worked as farmers, just as they had in Ireland, although they faced difficulties in adapting to the new land and climate.

By 1861, Cathrine would have been an established member of the Presbyterian faith community in Storrington, living the life of a settler in a rural farming community. Life would have been marked by hard work on the farm, maintaining family life, and adapting to a new country, far from her homeland in Ireland.

In summary, Cathrine McWatters was born in a politically tumultuous time in Ireland. Her early years would have been shaped by hardship, poverty, and the struggles of her people. The significant changes in Ireland and the promise of a better life in Canada would have likely motivated her to emigrate. Once in Storrington, Ontario, she would have experienced the challenges and rewards of farming in a new land, integrated into a tight-knit Presbyterian community, and continued her life in the aftermath of a difficult journey.

WHEN CATHRINE MCWATTERS was 6 years old, in 1807, the first successful commercial steamboat, The Clermont, was launched by Robert Fulton.

This event marked a major technological milestone in transportation. The Clermont successfully navigated the Hudson River in New York, demonstrating the potential of steam-powered boats for commercial travel. Before the steamboat, travel by water relied on sails or human power, which limited efficiency and speed. Fulton's steamboat revolutionized both trade and travel, paving the way for steamboats to become a key part of global transportation networks throughout the 19th century.

At the time, Cathrine, living in Ireland, would not have had direct contact with the new technology, but the success of steam travel in North America would have inspired the growing industrialization that was taking place worldwide. However, in rural Ireland, life would have remained relatively unchanged in the immediate years following the launch of the steamboat. Nonetheless, the invention was part of the broader technological shift that would eventually lead to major transformations in transportation and commerce in both the British Isles and the rest of the world.

WHEN CATHRINE MCWATTERS was 25 years old, in 1826, matches were invented by John Walker, an English chemist. Walker's invention was the first friction match, which ignited when struck against a rough surface. This invention revolutionized fire-starting methods, moving away from the cumbersome use of flint and steel.

Before the invention of matches, people relied on firesteels or flint to start fires, which was not only labor-intensive but also dangerous. The introduction of matches made lighting a fire more convenient and accessible, marking a significant advancement in everyday life.

In 1826, life in Ireland would still have been primarily agricultural, and technological innovations like matches, though impactful, would have been adopted more slowly in rural areas. However, by the time of her later years, Cathrine would likely have seen matches become common household items, providing greater ease in daily life.

ECHOES OF STORRINGTON

WHEN CATHRINE MCWATTERS was 38 years old, in 1839, the Irish Hurricane struck. This event was a rare and powerful tropical storm that caused extensive damage in Ireland. The storm, which occurred in early November, affected many parts of the country, particularly the south and east. It was considered one of the most devastating hurricanes to hit Ireland in recorded history.

For Cathrine, living in rural Ireland at the time, this would have been a significant event. The hurricane caused widespread destruction, especially to crops, homes, and infrastructure, which likely had a lasting economic impact on the community. In an era before modern weather forecasting, such storms would have been terrifying, and the aftermath would have left many communities struggling to rebuild.

Cathrine, being 38 years old, would have been an adult at this time, possibly managing her household and caring for any children. The hurricane would have been a reminder of the vulnerability of rural life, where extreme weather could change the course of lives and livelihoods.

AT 44 YEARS OLD, IN 1845, Cathrine McWatters would have experienced the start of the Irish Potato Famine, which spurred the mass Irish immigration to places like North America, particularly Canada, the United States, and Australia.

In Ireland, this was a deeply challenging time as the potato crop, a staple food for the Irish, failed due to a fungal disease known as potato blight. This caused widespread hunger, hardship, and death. The Great Famine would last from 1845 to 1852, and over a million people died from starvation and disease, while over a million more emigrated to escape the devastation.

For Cathrine, living through these events, the situation would have been grim. In rural communities like the one she likely inhabited, survival became precarious as the population faced extreme poverty. During this time, Irish immigration became an important and urgent response to the crisis. People like Cathrine might have witnessed friends, neighbors, and family members making the difficult decision to emigrate in search of a better life, often enduring harsh and perilous journeys.

In Canada, Irish immigrants, including those fleeing the famine, began arriving in large numbers. The influx of immigrants greatly impacted communities and reshaped the social and economic landscape, particularly in places like Ontario, where Cathrine might have been living by that time. The hardship brought on by the famine and the emigration it caused would likely have deeply affected her and her community.

IN 1861, AT 60 YEARS old, Cathrine McWatters would have witnessed significant changes, both personally and in the broader context of Storrington, Ontario. By then, she had likely been living in Ontario for many years, perhaps since the Irish immigration in the mid-19th century, when many Irish people fled the Potato Famine and came to Canada.

Being Catholic in a predominantly Protestant area like Storrington during this period would have placed her in a minority group. The social fabric of rural Ontario at the time was influenced by both the settlers of Anglo-Saxon descent and the growing number of Irish immigrants, many of whom were Catholic. The tensions between Catholics and Protestants were sometimes quite visible, especially in areas where Irish Catholic communities settled. However, by 1861, Storrington was a part of Ontario, which was rapidly developing and seeing shifts in its social structure as it became a haven for various immigrant groups, including the Irish.

At 60 years old, Cathrine would have experienced many hardships, including the death of family members, possibly due to the earlier years of the Potato Famine, as well as the challenges of aging without the support of a spouse or children to care for her. In her time, life expectancy was generally lower, and without the support of a partner, women often had to rely on their community, family, or faith for assistance. Given that she was single, it's possible that her Catholic faith played an even greater role in her life as a source of comfort, community, and strength.

Life in Storrington, a rural community, would have been focused on farming and self-sufficiency. As a widow in her 60s, Cathrine might have relied on her own farming efforts, or possibly those of extended family members. As a Catholic, she would have attended the local Catholic church and possibly been part of a smaller, tight-knit community.

In 1861, Canada was just a few years away from becoming a Dominion, with Confederation happening in 1867. However, in 1861, it was still very much a collection of British colonies. In this setting, her life would have been influenced by the economic and social challenges of the time, along with the Catholic-Protestant dynamics and the aftermath of the Irish immigration experience.

GENEALOGY ITINERARY:

Day 1: Arrival in Ontario

- Destination: Kingston, Ontario
- Activities:

- Check into a local hotel or bed and breakfast.

- Visit the Kingston Historical Society to gather preliminary information and resources about the region during the mid-19th century.

Day 2: Exploring Storrington

- Destination: Storrington, Ontario

- Activities:

- Visit the local archives or library to search for records related to Cathrine McWatters and her family.

- Explore the area to get a sense of the landscape and environment where Cathrine lived.

- Visit local Catholic churches to inquire about historical records and possibly view the church where Cathrine might have worshipped.

Day 3: Historical Research and Records

- Destination: Storrington, Ontario

- Activities:

- Spend the day at the local archives or library, focusing on census records, land records, and any other documents that might provide insights into Cathrine's life.

- Meet with local historians or genealogy groups to discuss your findings and get additional leads.

Day 4: Visiting Cemeteries and Historical Sites

- Destination: Storrington, Ontario

- Activities:

- Visit local cemeteries to find gravesites of Cathrine McWatters and her family members.

- Explore historical sites and landmarks in the area to understand the context of Cathrine's life in the 1860s.

Day 5: Day Trip to Nearby Historical Locations

- Destination: Surrounding areas of Storrington

- Activities:

- Take a day trip to nearby towns and villages to explore additional archives, libraries, and historical societies.

- Visit any relevant museums or heritage sites that provide a broader understanding of life in Canada West during the 19th century.

Day 6: Reflection and Documentation

- Destination: Kingston, Ontario

- Activities:

- Return to Kingston to compile and document your findings.

- Visit the Kingston Frontenac Public Library for any final research and to use their genealogy resources.

- Reflect on the journey and prepare a summary of your discoveries to share with family members.

Day 7: Departure

- Destination: Home

- Activities:

- Check out of your accommodation and travel back home.

- Plan a family gathering to share the stories and information you uncovered about Cathrine McWatters.

THOMAS McWATTERS

T**HOMAS McWATERS**[26]

Thomas McWatters, born in Upper Canada in 1835, grew up during a period of significant development and change in what would later become Ontario. At the time, Upper Canada was under British rule, and the colony was still heavily focused on agriculture and settlement expansion.

Life in 1835:

Economy: Upper Canada was a primarily rural and agrarian society, with most families relying on farming as their main livelihood. Trade with the United States and Great Britain was growing, though transportation of goods was slow due to the lack of infrastructure.

Politics: The colony was under British control, with a government system that often caused frustration among settlers due to limited local representation. This would later lead to the Upper Canadian Rebellion in 1837, when Thomas was just 2 years old.

Society: Life was hard but hopeful for settlers. They built communities centered around churches, schools, and marketplaces. Social activities often revolved around these institutions.

THOMAS'S FAMILY LIKELY worked hard to establish a stable life, clearing land for farming and building relationships within the local community.

AT 2 YEARS OLD, THOMAS McWatters was living in Upper Canada during the Upper and Lower Canadian Rebellions of 1837. These uprisings were driven by frustrations over the lack of responsible government and unequal distribution of land and power.

Impact on Life in 1837:

Upper Canadian Rebellion: Led by William Lyon Mackenzie, this rebellion aimed to reform political power structures and increase local governance. While it was short-lived and ultimately unsuccessful, it brought attention to the grievances of settlers.

Life for Families: For young families like the McWatters, the rebellion might have caused anxiety and disruptions, as many communities feared retaliation or unrest. However, rural families often remained focused on their farms and daily survival.

Aftermath: The rebellion eventually paved the way for political reform, leading to the establishment of responsible government in 1848, when Thomas was 13.

AT HIS YOUNG AGE, THOMAS would not have understood the political upheaval, but his family might have discussed the events or been indirectly affected by them.

AT 13 YEARS OLD, THOMAS McWatters witnessed a significant political development in Canada with the establishment of the principle of responsible government in 1848. This reform marked a turning point in Canadian governance, where the colonial government became accountable to the elected assembly rather than the British-appointed governor.

Context of 1848:

What It Meant: Responsible government allowed colonies like the Province of Canada (which included Upper and Lower Canada) to self-govern in matters of local concern, laying the groundwork for Canadian democracy.

Impact on Daily Life: For a farm boy like Thomas, this likely had little immediate effect on his day-to-day life. However, it marked a shift in the rights and representation of people in rural areas, including his family, within the political system.

Public Sentiment: Discussions about politics and reforms may have been a topic of conversation among adults in his community, especially as they considered how it might benefit farmers and settlers.

WHILE THOMAS MAY NOT have fully grasped the significance at the time, this milestone would shape the future of the land he called home.

IN 1861, THOMAS MCWATTERS was a 26-year-old farmer living in Storrington, Ontario. He was married, Presbyterian, and part of a growing rural community.

Life in Storrington, Ontario (1861):

Farming Lifestyle: As a farmer, Thomas's daily routine would have revolved around tending crops, caring for livestock, and managing his household. Farming in the mid-19th century was labor-intensive, relying on simple tools and techniques.

Presbyterian Faith: His Presbyterian faith would have played a central role in his life, with Sundays reserved for church services and family gatherings. The church would have been a hub for social and spiritual life.

Community Dynamics: Storrington was a small, rural township. Neighbors likely supported each other with communal efforts during harvests or barn-raisings, fostering a tight-knit community.

Census Insight: The 1861 census reveals a snapshot of families and occupations in the area, highlighting the agrarian nature of life.

THOMAS WAS PART OF a generation transitioning into a more structured Canadian society, balancing traditional ways with emerging advancements and governance in Canada West.

MARY (UNKNOWN) McWATTERS

MARY (UNKNOWN) McWATTERS[27]

Mary McWatters, born in Ireland in 1837, likely experienced significant transitions in her life before settling in Storrington, Ontario. Her maiden name remains a mystery, but her move to Canada West suggests she was part of the broader Irish immigration wave of the mid-19th century.

Life in Ireland (1837):

Social Context: The year Mary was born, Ireland was marked by increasing poverty and rural hardship. The economy was heavily agrarian, and tenant farming under absentee landlords dominated.

Population Growth: Ireland was densely populated, with limited resources, setting the stage for the famine that would strike a decade later.

British Rule: Ireland was under British governance, with growing calls for political reform and Irish self-determination.

LIKELY JOURNEY TO CANADA:

Mary likely emigrated as a child or young adult, possibly during or shortly after the Great Famine (1845–1852). The promise of land and a better life in Canada West (modern Ontario) drew many Irish families.

In 1861:

Age and Status: By 1861, Mary was 24 years old, Presbyterian, and married to Thomas McWatters, living in Storrington, Ontario.

Community Role: As a farmer's wife, she would have taken on significant responsibilities, including managing the household, raising children, and possibly helping with farm work.

Presbyterian Faith: Her adherence to Presbyterianism suggests either a shared faith background with her husband or a conversion, common among Irish immigrants integrating into predominantly Scottish-Presbyterian communities in Canada.

MARY'S STORY REFLECTS the resilience of Irish immigrants adapting to new lives while contributing to the development of rural Canada.

MARY MCWATTERS (BORN in 1837) was 8 years old during the Irish immigration of 1845, which marked the beginning of a mass exodus from Ireland due to the Great Famine.

1845 and Mary's Childhood:

Irish Context: The famine started with the potato blight, devastating the primary food source for much of Ireland's population. Starvation and disease began to spread, prompting many families to emigrate.

Family Decisions: If Mary emigrated during or shortly after this period, her family likely faced severe hardship, motivating them to seek opportunities abroad. Young children like Mary would have endured the uncertainty of long voyages and the challenges of starting anew in a foreign land.

BROADER IMPACT:

The Irish immigration of 1845 brought thousands to Canada, especially to Upper Canada (now Ontario), where communities of Irish settlers expanded. This wave reshaped Canadian society, with Irish immigrants influencing local culture, religion, and labor.

BY 1861, MARY MCWATTERS, born in Ireland in 1837, was 24 years old, Presbyterian, and married to Thomas McWatters. The couple lived in Storrington, Ontario, where Thomas worked as a farmer.

Life in Storrington, 1861:

Community: Storrington Township was a rural area with a mix of Irish, Scottish, and English settlers. Presbyterians like Mary were part of a significant religious group, often gathering in local churches that served as both spiritual and social hubs.

Daily Life: Mary likely managed household duties, which included cooking, preserving food, weaving, sewing, and assisting with farm tasks during busy seasons.

Immigrant Experience: Coming from Ireland, Mary would have brought traditions from her homeland, blending them into the community life in Canada West. The resilience of Irish immigrants was a defining trait, especially among women who adapted to frontier challenges.

MARY'S STORY REFLECTS the perseverance of Irish immigrants who forged new lives in Canada during the mid-19th century.

JOHN ISRAEL JOHNSTON

J OHN ISRAEL JOHNSTON[28]

John Johnston's birth year, 1811, places him in a period of significant change in Ireland and beyond. This was a time when Ireland was still under British rule, and tensions between the Irish population and the British government were growing. Here's a bit of context for the time:

Early 1800s in Ireland: The Act of Union in 1801 had merged the Kingdom of Ireland with Great Britain, creating the United Kingdom of Great Britain and Ireland. This union sparked unrest, especially among Irish nationalists who sought independence. The Rebellions of 1798 were still fresh in people's minds, and the Catholic Emancipation movement was gaining momentum, advocating for rights for Catholics, who had been marginalized under British laws.

1811: The early 19th century saw a growing industrial revolution in Britain, but Ireland remained largely rural and agricultural. The economy was still mainly focused on farming, and the growing population placed significant pressure on the land. Much of Ireland's land was owned by Anglo-Irish landlords, and the Irish tenants often faced difficult living conditions.

Political and Religious Tensions: This was also a time of significant political upheaval. The Catholic Relief Act of 1829, passed shortly after John's birth, granted some civil rights to Catholics in Ireland, but tensions between the Catholic majority and Protestant minority remained high. The Irish Rebellion of 1798 was still a memory, and many Irish Catholics continued to demand greater autonomy and rights.

Family Life: John would have grown up in a country where family life was often centered around agriculture, with people working the land. His early years would have been marked by the struggles of life in a colonial country. His childhood was likely influenced by the social hierarchy and the growing divide between the Irish Catholic peasants and the Protestant landowners.

AS AN ADULT IN THE 1830s and 1840s, John would have seen the economic hardships in Ireland, which eventually culminated in the Great Famine (1845–1852). Depending on his personal circumstances, he may have been one of the many Irish immigrants who sought a new life in Canada to escape the devastating famine and the accompanying poverty and starvation that ravaged Ireland.

His decision to immigrate to Canada (if he did) would likely have been driven by these hardships, and by the promise of land and freedom that Canada offered, particularly for the Irish. Many Irish immigrants came to Upper Canada (now Ontario) in the mid-19th century, and their experiences would shape the communities they formed.

If John was among the many Irish immigrants who arrived in Canada during or after the Irish Famine, his life would have been shaped by both the struggles in Ireland and the opportunities in his new country.

WHEN MATCHES WERE INVENTED in 1826, John Johnston would have been 15 years old. This was a period of significant technological progress, and the invention of matches was a notable part of it.

At the time, the friction match was invented by John Walker, an English chemist, who accidentally discovered how to make matches by scraping a stick of wood coated with chemicals along a rough surface. These early matches, known as "Congreves," were different from modern matches, requiring a rough surface to ignite them.

In Ireland, people were still largely dependent on methods like flint and steel or firestones to start fires. The introduction of matches would have had a considerable impact on everyday life, making it easier to light fires, which were crucial for heating, cooking, and lighting, especially in rural households.

For John, growing up in Ireland during this time, the invention of the match would have been a part of the broader advancements of the Industrial Revolution, bringing new tools and technologies into common use, including innovations that were reaching even remote areas of Ireland. This invention would have gradually changed how people interacted with fire in everyday life, making it much more accessible and safe compared to previous methods.

IN 1839, WHEN THE IRISH Hurricane struck, John Johnston would have been 28 years old. This hurricane was one of the most devastating natural disasters in Irish history, causing widespread destruction along the southern coast of Ireland.

The storm, which occurred in late November, is said to have affected Ireland for several days, bringing gale-force winds and torrential rain. It resulted in significant loss of life and property, particularly in Cork and Waterford. In the years leading up to the hurricane, Ireland was already experiencing economic difficulties, including the aftermath of the Great Famine, and the hurricane added to the hardships faced by many families.

John, living in Ireland during this time, would have witnessed or heard stories of the storm's impact, which might have left lasting effects on the community. If he lived in a coastal area, the hurricane would have directly affected him or those around him, possibly damaging homes, ships, and infrastructure.

IN 1845, WHEN IRISH immigration began due to the Great Famine, John Johnston would have been 34 years old. This was a pivotal moment in Irish history, as the famine, caused by a potato blight, led to mass starvation and widespread disease. The migration of Irish people to places like North America, Britain, and Australia increased dramatically during this time.

John, at 34, may have been directly impacted by these events. Many Irish families, struggling to survive, made the difficult decision to leave their homeland in search of better opportunities. It's possible that John, or members of his family, might have been among those who emigrated, either out of necessity or seeking a new life in a less affected region.

Those who stayed behind in Ireland, like John, would have seen their communities change significantly as families and villages were decimated by both the famine and the subsequent emigration.

BY 1861, JOHN JOHNSTON was 50 years old, married, a Presbyterian, and a farmer living in Storrington, Ontario. This period in Canada was marked by growth and development, especially in regions like Ontario, where settlers from various parts of the world, including Ireland, were establishing farms and communities.

For John, as a Presbyterian living in Storrington, he would have been part of a close-knit, religious community, with churches serving as important social and cultural hubs. Given his age and farming background, it's likely that John had already established a stable life in Canada by 1861, following a period of adjustment after his emigration from Ireland. The 1860s in Ontario also saw the expansion of agriculture, infrastructure, and local economies, so John may have been involved in these developments as a farmer.

His life would have been shaped by the challenges of farming in a new land, the impact of religious and cultural communities, and the ongoing growth of Canada West into what would later become Ontario.

GENEALOGY ITINERARY:

Day 1: Arrival in Ontario

- Destination: Kingston, Ontario

- Activities:

- Check into a local hotel or bed and breakfast.

- Visit the Kingston Historical Society to gather preliminary information and resources about the region during the mid-19th century.

Day 2: Exploring Storrington

- Destination: Storrington, Ontario

- Activities:

- Visit the local archives or library to search for records related to John Johnston and his farming activities.

- Explore the area to get a sense of the landscape and environment where John lived and worked.

- Visit local Presbyterian churches to inquire about historical records and possibly view the church where John and his family might have worshipped.

Day 3: Historical Research and Records

- Destination: Storrington, Ontario

- Activities:

- Spend the day at the local archives or library, focusing on census records, land records, and any other documents that might provide insights into John's life as a farmer.

- Meet with local historians or genealogy groups to discuss your findings and get additional leads.

Day 4: Visiting Cemeteries and Historical Sites

- Destination: Storrington, Ontario

- Activities:

- Visit local cemeteries to find gravesites of John Johnston and his family members.

[Sandhill Cemetery, South Frontenac, Frontenac, Ontario, Canada | BillionGraves Cemetery and Images](#)[1]

- EXPLORE HISTORICAL sites and landmarks in the area to understand the context of John's life in the 1860s.

Day 5: Day Trip to Nearby Historical Locations

- Destination: Surrounding areas of Storrington

---

1. https://billiongraves.com/cemetery/Sandhill-Cemetery/339618/volunteer

- Activities:

- Take a day trip to nearby towns and villages to explore additional archives, libraries, and historical societies.

- Visit any relevant museums or heritage sites that provide a broader understanding of life in Canada West during the 19th century.

Day 6: Reflection and Documentation

- Destination: Kingston, Ontario

- Activities:

- Return to Kingston to compile and document your findings.

- Visit the Kingston Frontenac Public Library for any final research and to use their genealogy resources.

- Reflect on the journey and prepare a summary of your discoveries to share with family members.

Day 7: Departure

- Destination: Home

- Activities:

- Check out of your accommodation and travel back home.

- Plan a family gathering to share the stories and information you uncovered about John Johnston.

SARAH MIRIAM (GORDON) JOHNSTON

SARAH MIRIAM (GORDON) JOHNSTON[29]

Sarah Johnston was born in Ireland in 1821, a period marked by significant social, political, and economic changes. Here's a glimpse of what life might have been like in Ireland during that time:

1. Political and Social Context

Post-Napoleonic Ireland: Ireland was under British rule, and its political situation was turbulent. The Act of Union (1801) had formally merged the Kingdom of Ireland with Great Britain, creating the United Kingdom of Great Britain and Ireland. However, this union did not quell Irish dissatisfaction, and many Irish people, especially Catholics, were frustrated by their lack of political representation and civil rights.

The Catholic Emancipation: In 1829, Ireland saw the Catholic Emancipation Act, which allowed Catholics to sit in the British Parliament for the first time. Though this came after Sarah's birth, it was a significant shift in Irish political dynamics that influenced the climate during her early years.

Ongoing Poverty and Inequality: The vast majority of Irish people lived in poverty. The majority were tenant farmers on land owned by English or Anglo-Irish landlords, subject to rent payments and harsh living conditions. Economic inequality was stark, and many struggled to make a living.

2. ECONOMIC LANDSCAPE

Agricultural Economy: Ireland's economy was primarily agricultural, with the majority of people working on small farms growing crops like potatoes, barley, wheat, and oats. The early 19th century was a time of agricultural development, but the country's dependence on the potato crop would have lasting negative consequences, as the crop failed in the coming decades.

Economic Hardships: Though the potato was a staple food, Ireland's economy was still fragile, and the reliance on a single crop made the country vulnerable to famine. By 1821, the Irish were already suffering from economic hardship, with land ownership concentrated in the hands of the few and many others living as tenant farmers on rented land.

---

3. SOCIAL LIFE

Rural vs. Urban Living: Most of Ireland's population lived in rural areas, like where Sarah would have been born. Cities like Dublin, Cork, and Belfast were growing, but rural life was still the norm. People lived in small, modest homes, often made of stone or mud with thatched roofs. In the countryside, families tended to large animals, grew crops, and lived off the land.

The Role of Women: Women in 1821 were typically responsible for domestic duties, such as cooking, cleaning, child-rearing, and helping with the agricultural work. For those in rural areas, women were often integral to farming activities, especially tasks like milking cows, tending to gardens, and processing food.

---

4. RELIGIOUS INFLUENCE

Predominantly Catholic: Ireland in 1821 was predominantly Catholic, with Protestantism mostly confined to the Anglo-Irish elite. The Catholic church held significant influence over many aspects of daily life, including education, social services, and even politics.

Religious Tensions: There were tensions between the Catholic majority and the Protestant minority, particularly in Northern Ireland, which would intensify later in the century. However, for much of the country, religious identity was closely linked to Irish national identity.

5. CULTURAL CONTEXT

Language and Tradition: Irish Gaelic was still widely spoken, especially in rural areas, though English was increasingly used for government and trade. Irish culture was rich in folklore, music, and oral traditions, with a strong connection to the land and community.

Education: Education was not widely accessible, particularly in rural areas. However, hedge schools (informal schools run by private tutors) were common, and many children, especially in the countryside, learned from their parents and community.

6. THE ROAD TO FAMINE

While 1821 was a time of relative peace in Ireland, it was also a period leading up to significant hardship. The early 19th century would later give way to the Great Irish Famine (1845-1852), which had catastrophic consequences. The overreliance on the potato, coupled with a series of crop failures, would lead to mass starvation and emigration during Sarah's later life.

IN SHORT, IRELAND IN 1821 was a time of economic struggles, social inequality, and political unrest. It was a society heavily influenced by British colonial rule and the Catholic Church, with an agricultural economy that would soon face major upheavals.

WHEN SARAH JOHNSTON was 5 years old in 1826, the first friction match was invented. This event is significant because it marked the beginning of a new era in convenience and safety for lighting fires, which had previously been much more cumbersome and dangerous.

What Life Was Like in 1826:

The Invention of the Friction Match: In 1826, the English chemist John Walker created the first friction match, which he initially sold as "lucifers." Unlike earlier forms of matches, these could be struck against a rough surface to ignite. This invention made it easier for people to start fires for cooking, warmth, and light, a major advancement compared to using flint and steel or other methods.

Life in Ireland: At this time, Ireland was still under British rule, and much of its population lived in rural areas, working the land. The economy was largely agrarian, and people relied on traditional methods to meet their daily needs. The invention of matches would have likely made life a bit easier for those living in more isolated parts of Ireland, including Sarah's family, as it would have been much more practical than previous methods of starting fires.

MATCHES REPRESENTED a small, but important, step in the modernization of everyday life. Though it wouldn't immediately transform life in rural Ireland, it would gradually spread and be adopted, making fire-starting safer and more accessible, especially for those who had limited resources.

IN 1839, WHEN SARAH Johnston was 18 years old, the Irish Hurricane occurred, which was one of the most devastating storms in Irish history. Known as "The Big Wind," it swept through Ireland on January 6, 1839, and caused widespread destruction.

Impact of the Irish Hurricane (The Big Wind):

Destruction: The storm caused massive damage to homes, farms, and infrastructure. It destroyed thousands of houses, uprooted trees, and damaged crops, leading to severe economic losses. Many areas were left without shelter or resources, especially in rural Ireland, where the majority of the population lived.

Casualties: Although the exact number of deaths is uncertain, it is estimated that the hurricane caused the deaths of at least 300 people across Ireland. The destruction of property and infrastructure made recovery difficult for many.

Sarah's Experience: As an 18-year-old living in Ireland, Sarah would have witnessed the full scale of the storm's devastation, especially if she lived in a rural area. The storm would have had a profound impact on daily life, making it harder to gather food and supplies, and potentially displacing many people from their homes. The damage to agriculture could have caused financial hardship, affecting families like Sarah's who might have relied on farming.

THE HURRICANE WAS A powerful reminder of the vulnerability of rural Ireland to extreme weather, and the hardship it brought would have contributed to the ongoing social and economic struggles of the time. For Sarah and her community, the storm would have likely been a defining event in her young adulthood, reshaping the local landscape and perhaps altering the course of her family's life.

IN 1845, WHEN SARAH Johnston was 24 years old, the Great Irish Famine began, which triggered one of the most significant waves of Irish immigration. The famine was caused by a potato blight that devastated Ireland's staple crop, leading to mass starvation and disease. The effects were profound, causing Ireland's population to plummet due to death and emigration.

Impact of the Irish Immigration of 1845:

The Famine's Cause: The potato blight arrived in Ireland in 1845, and by the following year, it wiped out a majority of the potato crop. Potatoes were the primary food source for much of the Irish population, particularly the poor. With crops failing, a severe food shortage ensued.

Mass Emigration: By the mid-1840s, the famine forced many Irish people to leave their homeland in search of a better life. Over a million people died from starvation and disease, while over 2 million emigrated, primarily to the United States, Canada, and other parts of the British Empire.

Sarah's Experience: At 24, Sarah would have witnessed firsthand the devastating impact of the famine on her community. If she was living in a rural area, her family likely struggled with food shortages and the loss of their primary crop. Like many others, Sarah and her family may have faced difficult decisions about whether to stay and try to survive or join the wave of emigrants leaving for places like Canada, which was offering free land to settlers.

The Decision to Emigrate: Sarah may have been part of the great migration to Canada. The promise of land and a fresh start was appealing to many Irish families who were facing poverty, disease, and hunger. It was common for entire families or communities to emigrate together, and they often faced perilous journeys across the Atlantic, arriving in Canada with little more than the hope of a new life.

THE YEAR 1845, MARKING the onset of the Irish Famine and the beginning of mass emigration, would have been a turning point for Sarah and her family, likely shaping her future. If she did emigrate, the experience of leaving Ireland during such a tragic period would have been deeply significant.

IN 1861, SARAH JOHNSTON, at 40 years old, would have been living in Storrington, Ontario with her husband, John Johnston. As a Presbyterian, Sarah's faith would likely have played an important role in her life, offering community support and comfort as she settled into her new life in Canada.

Life in 1861:

Immigration and Settlement: By 1861, Sarah and her husband John would have been settled in Ontario for several years. If they had immigrated during the Irish Famine in the 1840s, they would have been part of the many Irish immigrants who sought refuge in Canada, which was viewed as a place of opportunity amidst the devastating famine back home. The couple may have faced the typical challenges of early Canadian settlers, such as establishing a farm, adapting to a new environment, and building relationships with neighbors in a predominantly agricultural society.

Family and Faith: Sarah, as a mother or potentially a homemaker, would have been involved in raising children and maintaining a household in rural Ontario. The Presbyterian faith, with its strong emphasis on community and worship, would have provided a sense of stability and belonging. If Sarah attended church services, she would have been part of a tight-knit community that supported each other through the hardships of pioneer life.

Economic Life: As a farmer and Presbyterian, Sarah's husband, John, would have likely worked the land in Ontario. With the introduction of new agricultural techniques and the availability of land grants, the couple might have had a modest but stable life by 1861. They would have been part of the agricultural backbone of Ontario's economy, growing crops and raising livestock to sustain their family.

Social and Cultural Life: As Presbyterians, Sarah and John would have been part of a Protestant community in a predominantly Anglican and Catholic Ontario. Religion would have been central to their social life, providing regular worship opportunities and a community of like-minded individuals. They would have also likely been involved in social events such as barn raisings, local fairs, and other community gatherings that helped forge connections in their new home.

Canada in 1861: In 1861, Canada was still a British colony, and life for settlers in Ontario was centered around agriculture and small communities. The population was growing, and towns like Kingston and Toronto were becoming hubs of trade and communication. The Province of Canada (now Ontario and Quebec) was still part of the broader British Empire, and Confederation—when Canada would unite as a country—was still a few years away (1867).

OVERALL, SARAH'S LIFE in 1861 would have been marked by her strong Presbyterian faith, a stable farming life with her husband, and the ongoing adjustments of living as an immigrant in a developing Canadian society.

GENEALOGY ITINERARY:

Day 1: Arrival in Ontario

- Destination: Kingston, Ontario

- Activities:

- Check into a local hotel or bed and breakfast.

- Visit the Kingston Historical Society to gather preliminary information and resources about the region during the mid-19th century.

Day 2: Exploring Storrington

- Destination: Storrington, Ontario

- Activities:

- Visit the local archives or library to search for records related to Sarah Johnston and her family.

- Explore the area to get a sense of the landscape and environment where Sarah lived.

- Visit local Presbyterian churches to inquire about historical records and possibly view the church where Sarah and her family might have worshipped.

Day 3: Historical Research and Records

- Destination: Storrington, Ontario

- Activities:

- Spend the day at the local archives or library, focusing on census records, land records, and any other documents that might provide insights into Sarah's life as a farmer's wife.

- Meet with local historians or genealogy groups to discuss your findings and get additional leads.

Day 4: Visiting Cemeteries and Historical Sites

- Destination: Storrington, Ontario

- Activities:

- Visit local cemeteries to find gravesites of Sarah Johnston and her family members.

Sandhill Cemetery, South Frontenac, Frontenac, Ontario, Canada | BillionGraves Cemetery and Images[1]

- EXPLORE HISTORICAL sites and landmarks in the area to understand the context of Sarah's life in the 1860s.

Day 5: Day Trip to Nearby Historical Locations

- Destination: Surrounding areas of Storrington

- Activities:

- Take a day trip to nearby towns and villages to explore additional archives, libraries, and historical societies.

---

1. https://billiongraves.com/cemetery/Sandhill-Cemetery/339618/volunteer

- Visit any relevant museums or heritage sites that provide a broader understanding of life in Canada West during the 19th century.

Day 6: Reflection and Documentation

- Destination: Kingston, Ontario

- Activities:

- Return to Kingston to compile and document your findings.

- Visit the Kingston Frontenac Public Library for any final research and to use their genealogy resources.

- Reflect on the journey and prepare a summary of your discoveries to share with family members.

Day 7: Departure

- Destination: Home

- Activities:

- Check out of your accommodation and travel back home.

- Plan a family gathering to share the stories and information you uncovered about Sarah Johnston.

JAMES JOHNSTON

JAMES JOHNSTON[30]
James Johnston's Life in 1843

Born in Upper Canada (now Ontario) in 1843, James Johnston came into the world during a period of rapid growth and social change. His parents, John and Sarah, were Irish immigrants who had settled in the colony, likely seeking a better life. As settlers, they were part of a growing population in a region defined by its agricultural economy, scattered communities, and emerging infrastructure.

What Was Happening in Upper Canada in 1843?

Economic Development: Upper Canada was primarily agrarian, with most families, including James's, living on farms. This was also the period when the region saw improvements in transportation, such as roads and canals, which facilitated trade and settlement.

Irish Immigration: Though the Irish Famine had not yet occurred, Irish immigration was already significant in the 1830s and 1840s due to political unrest and economic hardship in Ireland. Families like the Johnstons contributed to the growing Irish presence in Upper Canada.

Religion and Community: As Presbyterians, James's family would have been part of a Protestant community in a colony where Anglicans and Catholics were more prevalent. Church life was central to social and spiritual well-being, with regular worship and gatherings providing support for settlers.

JAMES IN HIS EARLY Years

As a baby in 1843, James would have been raised on a farm, surrounded by the labor and daily routines of rural life. He would have grown up helping his parents and siblings with chores and learning the skills needed to manage a homestead. The Johnstons would have emphasized religious faith, instilling in James the Presbyterian values of discipline, hard work, and community service.

Historical Context

Responsible Government: The political climate in Upper Canada was evolving. In the years following the Rebellions of 1837-38, reforms were introduced, including the gradual establishment of responsible government, which was officially recognized in 1848.

Population Growth: The colony's population was expanding due to immigration, creating more opportunities for settlers like the Johnstons but also leading to challenges like land disputes and competition for resources.

IN 1848, WHEN JAMES Johnston was 5 years old, the Principle of Responsible Government was established in Canada, marking a significant step toward democracy. This principle meant that the executive council (essentially the government) was accountable to the elected assembly, not the appointed governor, shifting political power toward the people.

What Did This Mean for James's World in 1848?

Political Stability: The political reforms reduced tensions following the Rebellions of 1837-38. While James, as a child, might not have understood these changes, his parents would have seen this as a hopeful sign of fairness and better governance in their new homeland.

Life on the Farm: For James, the principle of responsible government didn't immediately impact his daily life. He was likely busy with farm chores, education (if accessible), and church activities. However, the reforms set the stage for a more inclusive society, ensuring that settlers like his family had a voice in the decisions affecting their lives.

THIS POLITICAL MILESTONE represented progress in the colony where James was growing up, offering hope for a stable and prosperous future for immigrant families like the Johnstons.

IN 1861, JAMES JOHNSTON was 18 years old, a Presbyterian, and working as a farmer while living with his parents, John and Sarah Johnston, in Storrington, Ontario. As a young adult during this time, James would have been a vital part of the family farm's labor force.

What Life Was Like for an 18-Year-Old Farmer in 1861:

Farming Responsibilities: James likely helped with plowing fields, planting crops, tending livestock, and harvesting. Farming life was demanding, and every family member contributed to ensure survival and productivity.

Religious Life: As a Presbyterian, James and his family would have observed the Sabbath strictly, attended church regularly, and participated in community events tied to their faith.

Social Opportunities: Living in a rural area, James's social circle would have been small but active within the local Presbyterian community.

Social events often revolved around the church, barn-raisings, and seasonal celebrations.

Education and Literacy: By 1861, schooling in rural areas like Storrington was often limited. If James had attended a local schoolhouse, his education might have ended early as farm work took precedence. However, he may have been literate, particularly in reading the Bible.

Political Awareness: While not yet of voting age (21), James might have been aware of debates surrounding Canadian Confederation, which would occur in a few years.

FOR JAMES, LIFE IN Storrington was centered on family, faith, and farm duties, with limited leisure but a strong sense of community and purpose.

GENEALOGY ITINERARY:

Day 1: Arrival in Kingston, Ontario

- Morning: Arrive in Kingston, Ontario. Check into your accommodation.

- Afternoon: Visit Kingston City Hall, a historic building that offers insights into the local history and governance during James Johnston's time.

City Hall | City of Kingston[1]

- EVENING: ENJOY A leisurely dinner at a local restaurant and explore downtown Kingston.

1. https://www.cityofkingston.ca/arts-culture-and-events/history-and-heritage/city-hall/

Day 2: Exploring Storrington and Surroundings

• Morning: Drive to Storrington, South Frontenac Place:Storrington, Frontenac, Ontario, Canada - Genealogy[2]

Start with a visit to the area where James Johnston lived and farmed. Take a walk around the countryside to get a feel for the land he worked on.

• Afternoon: Visit Bedford Hall in Godfrey, a nearby historical site that offers a glimpse into the community life of the 19th century.

https://events.southfrontenac.net/default/Month?_mid_=5460

• EVENING: RETURN TO Kingston for dinner and relaxation.

Day 3: Historical and Cultural Insights

• Morning: Visit the Archives of Ontario in Toronto (if you can make the trip), where you can find historical records, land deeds, and other documents related to James Johnston and his family.

Heritage Property INdex » Storrington Township[3]

• AFTERNOON: EXPLORE the 1000 Islands History Museum in Gananoque, which provides a broader context of the region's history, including the era when James Johnston lived.

1000 Islands History Museum[4]

---

2. https://www.werelate.org/wiki/Place:Storrington%2C_Frontenac%2C_Ontario%2C_Canada

3. https://ontario.heritagepin.com/storrington-township-in-frontenac/

4. https://www.1000islandshistorymuseum.com/

- EVENING: ENJOY A scenic boat tour of the 1000 Islands, if weather permits.

Day 4: Presbyterian Heritage

- Morning: Visit a local Presbyterian Church in Kingston or the surrounding area to understand the religious context of James Johnston's life. Many churches have historical records and archives that might provide additional insights.

Presbyterian Church in Canada - Wikipedia[5]

- AFTERNOON: EXPLORE the Presbyterian Church in Canada Archives online or in person to find more about the church's history and its role in the community during the 19th century.

PRESBYTERY RECORDS[6]

- EVENING: REFLECT on the day's discoveries over dinner.

Day 5: Final Reflections and Departure

- Morning: Take a final walk around Kingston, perhaps visiting any remaining sites of interest or doing some last-minute research at local libraries or historical societies.

---

5. https://en.wikipedia.org/wiki/Presbyterian_Church_in_Canada

6. https://presbyterianarchives.ca/finding-aids/presbytery-records/

- Afternoon: Depart from Kingston, taking with you the rich history and memories of James Johnston's life and times.

This itinerary should give you a comprehensive view of James Johnston's life and the historical context in which he lived. Enjoy your journey into the past!

WILLIAM JOHNSTON

WILLIAM JOHNSTON[31]

William Johnston, born in 1849 in Canada West, was the younger brother of James Johnston and the son of John and Sarah Johnston. As the second son in a farming family, William would have grown up helping on the family farm, learning the necessary skills to eventually contribute fully to its operations.

Historical Context of 1849:

Canada West: Formerly Upper Canada, Canada West was part of the Province of Canada following the Act of Union in 1841. It was a time of growth, with infrastructure improvements like roads and canals helping to connect rural areas.

Education: By 1849, local school systems were being established in Canada West, although access in rural areas like Storrington could be sporadic.

IN HIS EARLY YEARS, William would have been surrounded by the rhythms of rural life, shaped by family, faith, and agricultural work.

IN 1861, WILLIAM JOHNSTON was 12 years old, Presbyterian, and living with his family in Storrington, Ontario. At this age, he likely assisted with light chores on the family farm, such as feeding animals, gathering firewood, or tending to the garden. His schooling, if available, would have been basic, focusing on reading, writing, arithmetic, and religious instruction.

Living in a rural, close-knit community, William's life would have revolved around family, church, and the seasonal demands of farm life. The Johnston family's Presbyterian faith would have played a significant role in their daily routines, including Sunday worship and community gatherings.

GENEALOGY ITINERARY

Day 1: Arrival in Kingston, Ontario

• Morning: Arrive in Kingston, Ontario. Check into your accommodation.

• Afternoon: Visit Kingston City Hall, a historic building that offers insights into the local governance and architecture during William Johnston's era.

CITY HALL | CITY OF Kingston[1]

• EVENING: ENJOY A leisurely dinner at a local restaurant and explore downtown Kingston.

Day 2: Exploring Storrington and Surroundings

• Morning: Drive to Storrington, South Frontenac. Start with a visit to the area where William Johnston lived. Walk around the countryside to get a feel for the land he grew up on.

Place:Storrington, Frontenac, Ontario, Canada - Genealogy[2]

---

1. https://www.cityofkingston.ca/arts-culture-and-events/history-and-heritage/city-hall/

- AFTERNOON: VISIT Bedford Hall in Godfrey, a nearby historical site that provides a glimpse into the community life of the 19th century.

https://events.southfrontenac.net/default/Month?_mid_=5460

- EVENING: RETURN TO Kingston for dinner and relaxation.

Day 3: Historical and Cultural Insights

- Morning: Visit the Archives of Ontario in Toronto (if you can make the trip), where you can find historical records, land deeds, and other documents related to William Johnston and his family.

SEARCH: BIRTHS, MARRIAGES and Deaths recorded in Canada - Library and Archives Canada[3]

- AFTERNOON: EXPLORE the 1000 Islands History Museum in Gananoque, which provides a broader context of the region's history, including the era when William Johnston lived.

1000 Islands History Museum[4]

---

2. https://www.werelate.org/wiki/Place:Storrington%2C_Frontenac%2C_Ontario%2C_Canada

3. https://www.bac-lac.gc.ca/eng/discover/vital-statistics-births-marriages-deaths/births-marriages-deaths-recorded/Pages/search.aspx

4. https://www.1000islandshistorymuseum.com/

- EVENING: ENJOY A scenic boat tour of the 1000 Islands, if weather permits.

Day 4: Presbyterian Heritage

- Morning: Visit a local Presbyterian Church in Kingston or the surrounding area to understand the religious context of William Johnston's life. Many churches have historical records and archives that might provide additional insights.

Presbyterian Church in Canada - Wikipedia[5]

- AFTERNOON: EXPLORE the Presbyterian Church in Canada Archives online or in person to find more about the church's history and its role in the community during the 19th century.

PRESBYTERY RECORDS[6]

- EVENING: REFLECT on the day's discoveries over dinner.

Day 5: Final Reflections and Departure

- Morning: Take a final walk around Kingston, perhaps visiting any remaining sites of interest or doing some last-minute research at local libraries or historical societies.

- Afternoon: Depart from Kingston, taking with you the rich history and memories of William Johnston's life and times.

---

5. https://en.wikipedia.org/wiki/Presbyterian_Church_in_Canada

6. https://presbyterianarchives.ca/finding-aids/presbytery-records/

This itinerary should give you a comprehensive view of William Johnston's life and the historical context in which he lived. Enjoy your journey into the past!

MARY SEREPTA JOHNSTON

MARY SEREPTA JOHNSTON[32]

Mary Johnston, born in 1847 in Canada West, was the daughter of John and Sarah Johnston. At the time of her birth, Canada West (modern-day Ontario) was experiencing growth and development, with settlers focusing on agriculture and the establishment of communities.

IN 1848, WHEN THE PRINCIPLE of Responsible Government was established, Mary Johnston was just 1 year old. This principle marked a significant shift in Canadian governance, granting elected officials more authority over colonial matters, and reducing the direct control of British-appointed governors.

Although Mary was too young to comprehend these changes, her parents, John and Sarah, might have been aware of the implications, especially as settlers adapting to life in a developing Canada West. The introduction of responsible government meant the beginning of a more democratic society, shaping the political landscape Mary would grow up in.

IN 1849, WHEN HER BROTHER William Johnston was born, Mary Johnston was 2 years old. At this time, the family lived in Canada West, a region undergoing significant growth and settlement. With the arrival of William, the Johnston household expanded, likely adding joy and more responsibilities for their parents, John and Sarah. As Mary grew older, she would have shared her early childhood experiences with her younger brother, forging a sibling bond amidst the rural life of 19th-century Ontario.

BY 1861, MARY WAS 14 years old, Presbyterian, and living in Storrington, Ontario, with her family. As a young girl in a farming household, her responsibilities would have included assisting with household chores like cooking, cleaning, sewing, and possibly helping care for younger siblings or tending to a vegetable garden. Her education would have been limited but sufficient to teach her basic literacy and numeracy, likely supplemented by Bible studies as part of her Presbyterian upbringing.

Mary's teenage years were shaped by rural life, community ties, and her family's faith, which provided a strong framework for her daily activities and future prospects.

SANDHILL CEMETERY, South Frontenac, Frontenac, Ontario, Canada | BillionGraves Cemetery and Images[1]

---

1. https://billiongraves.com/cemetery/Sandhill-Cemetery/339618/volunteer

ANNE JOHNSTON

A NNE JOHNSTON[33]

Anne Johnston, born in 1851 in Canada West, was the younger sister of Mary Johnston. Her birth came during a time of significant development and change in the region, as settlers continued to clear land, build farms, and establish communities. The family likely celebrated Anne's arrival, and as a middle child, Mary, at about 4 years old, may have helped care for her new baby sister, learning early lessons in responsibility and nurturing. Growing up together, Mary and Anne would have shared the experiences of rural childhood in the mid-19th century.

LIFE IN 1851, THE YEAR Anne Johnston was born, was shaped by significant social and economic developments across Canada West (now Ontario) and the broader world.

Canada West in 1851:

1. Population Growth: Immigration from Ireland and Scotland, driven by famine and economic hardship, was adding to the population of Canada West. Many immigrants sought opportunities in agriculture and settlement.

2. AGRICULTURAL ECONOMY: Rural families like Anne's lived off the land. Farming was the primary occupation, and families worked together to grow crops like wheat, oats, and potatoes, as well as raise livestock.

3. RELIGION AND COMMUNITY: Faith played a central role in community life. Presbyterian congregations, in particular, emphasized morality, education, and social cohesion.

4. DAILY LIFE: LIFE was labor-intensive, with tasks divided by gender. Women handled cooking, preserving food, sewing, and child-rearing, while men worked the fields and handled heavy labor. Children helped from a young age.

TECHNOLOGICAL AND SOCIAL Changes:

1. Infrastructure Development: Railways were beginning to connect towns and cities, although rural areas still relied heavily on horse-drawn transport and waterways.

2. COMMUNICATION: THE postal system was expanding, and newspapers were a primary source of information for those who could read.

3. INDUSTRIALIZATION: While much of Canada West remained agricultural, small industries and towns were growing, particularly near Kingston, Toronto, and other centers.

4. EDUCATION: PUBLIC education was developing, though attendance was irregular in rural areas due to the demands of farm life.

GLOBAL CONTEXT:

1. British Influence: Canada West was still a British colony, and ties to Britain influenced politics, trade, and culture.

2. CRIMEAN WAR BREWING: Although not directly involved, events leading to the Crimean War (1853-1856) highlighted global tensions.

IN THIS CONTEXT, ANNE'S family would have experienced both the challenges of rural life—hard work, seasonal cycles, and self-sufficiency—and the broader social changes shaping the region. Her early years would have been marked by community connections, faith-based traditions, and the gradual modernization of Canadian society.

IN 1861, ANNE JOHNSTON was 10 years old, Presbyterian, and living with her family in Storrington, Ontario. She would have been helping with chores around the farm and learning household skills from her mother, Sarah. Education was likely part of her routine, as Presbyterian communities often emphasized literacy and schooling. Her daily life would have revolved around family, faith, and the rhythms of rural living in a growing and industrious Canadian township.

JANE JOHNSTON

JANE JOHNSTON[34]

Jane Johnston, born in Canada West in 1853, arrived during a time of continued growth and transition in the region. Here's what life was like in 1853:

Canada West in 1853:

1. Expansion of Railways: The Grand Trunk Railway was under construction, aiming to connect key cities in Canada West and improve transportation and trade.

2. IMMIGRATION: THE influx of Irish immigrants continued, many settling in rural areas or small towns, contributing to a diverse cultural landscape.

3. AGRICULTURAL FOCUS: Most families, including Jane's, relied on farming. Life revolved around planting and harvesting crops, with an emphasis on self-sufficiency.

4. SETTLER LIFE: HOUSES were often made of wood or logs, and many families cooked over open hearths. Neighbors relied on each other for help during planting, harvesting, and emergencies.

SOCIAL AND CULTURAL Context:

1. Religion: Presbyterianism and other Christian denominations remained central to social and family life. Church attendance was common, and Sunday was a day of rest.

---

2. EDUCATION: PUBLIC schooling was available but not universally attended in rural areas due to farm labor demands. Girls like Jane often learned domestic skills at home.

---

3. FAMILY DYNAMICS: Large families were typical, with siblings contributing to household and farming chores. Jane would have grown up in a busy household with her older siblings helping to care for her.

TECHNOLOGICAL AND POLITICAL Climate:

1. Economic Growth: Trade was improving with infrastructure projects like railroads and canals, fostering connections between rural and urban areas.

---

2. RESPONSIBLE GOVERNMENT: Canada was transitioning politically after the establishment of responsible government in 1848, fostering greater autonomy in local governance.

---

3. GLOBAL EVENTS: THE Industrial Revolution was influencing technology and production, though its effects were felt more slowly in rural Canada.

DAILY LIFE FOR A YOUNG Family:

For a farming family like the Johnstons, 1853 would have been a year of routine and hard work. Jane's early years would be spent surrounded by the rhythms of rural life, strong family bonds, and the Presbyterian values her parents instilled in their children. As she grew, she would be shaped by these formative experiences and the steady changes in Canada West society.

IN 1861, JANE JOHNSTON was 8 years old, Presbyterian, and living with her family in Storrington, Ontario. Her daily life would have reflected the experiences of a young girl in a rural farming community during mid-19th century Canada.

Life as an 8-Year-Old Girl in 1861:

1. Family and Chores:

Jane likely had responsibilities around the household, such as helping her mother with cleaning, cooking, or watching over younger siblings.

On a farm, children were often expected to assist with light outdoor chores, such as feeding animals or gathering eggs.

2. EDUCATION:

If a school was nearby and accessible, Jane might have attended, learning basic reading, writing, and arithmetic.

Rural schooling was informal, with one-room schoolhouses accommodating children of all ages.

3. CHURCH AND RELIGION:

As a Presbyterian family, Sundays would have been devoted to church services and rest. Religious instruction was also common at home, with an emphasis on Bible study and moral lessons.

4. COMMUNITY LIFE:

Socializing happened at church gatherings, local markets, or community events.

Jane's family likely interacted with neighbors for mutual assistance and companionship in their close-knit community.

5. PLAY AND LEISURE:

Jane would have enjoyed simple games, storytelling, or exploring the countryside with her siblings and friends.

Toys were handmade and included items like dolls, hoops, or carved wooden figures.

Storrington in 1861:

Storrington was a rural township characterized by farming and small settlements. Life was relatively quiet, with a focus on agricultural productivity and maintaining a self-sufficient lifestyle.

For Jane, this time would have been defined by family bonds, the responsibilities of farm life, and the teachings of her Presbyterian faith, all while navigating the unique challenges and joys of childhood in a growing rural community.

ELIZABETH JOHNSTON

ELIZABETH JOHNSTON[35]

Elizabeth Johnston, born in Canada West in 1855, was the youngest daughter of John and Sarah Johnston at that time.

Life in Canada West in 1855:

The year of Elizabeth's birth saw ongoing growth and development in Canada West (now Ontario). Railways expanded, connecting towns and enabling the movement of goods and people. Agriculture was the mainstay for families, including the Johnstons, who lived in Storrington Township. Political discussions were also leading toward the confederation of Canada in 1867, though Elizabeth would have been too young to be aware of these changes.

Childhood in 1855:

As a baby, Elizabeth would have been cared for by her mother, Sarah, with help from older siblings like James, Mary, and William. Family life revolved around the farm and household, and her early years would have been spent in the close-knit environment of their rural community.

In 1861:

At 6 years old, Elizabeth was:

Presbyterian: Religion played a significant role in shaping her early education and moral upbringing.

Living in Storrington, Ontario: She shared her home with her parents, John and Sarah, and her siblings. The family farm likely provided most of their sustenance and was a central part of their daily lives.

Learning and Playing: By this age, she might have begun learning basic household tasks alongside her sisters while also enjoying the simple joys of childhood, like playing with handmade toys or exploring the surrounding farmland.

ELIZABETH'S UPBRINGING would have been deeply influenced by her family's Presbyterian faith, their agricultural lifestyle, and the rural community's close-knit culture.

IN 1861, ELIZABETH Johnston was 6 years old and living with her family in Storrington, Ontario. As a Presbyterian, her upbringing likely revolved around church activities and Sunday worship, which were central to her family's life.

At her young age, Elizabeth would have been learning the basics of life on the family farm. Her days were probably filled with helping her mother and older siblings with simple chores, such as gathering eggs or fetching water, while also having time to play with her siblings. The Johnston household was part of a growing agricultural community, and Elizabeth's life was typical of a rural upbringing in Canada West during this time.

The nearby township of Storrington offered a quiet but industrious environment where farming families like the Johnstons worked hard to sustain themselves, relying on local markets, churches, and schools for support and community interaction. Life was simple but demanding, and Elizabeth's childhood would have been deeply tied to her family's faith and work ethic.

JOHN LINDSAY

JOHN LINDSAY[36]

John Lindsay, born in Ireland in 1810, came into the world during a time of significant changes and challenges on the island.

Life in Ireland in 1810:

Agriculture: Ireland's economy was largely agrarian, with most people relying on farming. Tenant farmers worked the land owned by landlords, often under difficult conditions.

Society: The Penal Laws, restricting the rights of Catholics and Protestant dissenters, were being gradually relaxed, but the effects lingered.

Economy: The Napoleonic Wars (1803–1815) were in progress, impacting Ireland through increased demand for agricultural produce and military recruitment.

Transportation and Industry: The construction of canals and improved roads facilitated trade, though Ireland was still far less industrialized than Britain.

SIGNIFICANT EVENTS Around His Birth:

In 1801, the Act of Union had merged Ireland with Great Britain, creating the United Kingdom of Great Britain and Ireland.

The 1810s were marked by population growth, but also increasing strain on resources, laying the groundwork for future economic difficulties.

BY THE TIME JOHN EMIGRATED to Canada, he likely carried with him the resilience shaped by Ireland's social and economic challenges. His experiences would have been deeply influenced by the shifting tides of Irish and British history.

WHEN JOHN LINDSAY WAS 16 years old, in 1826, matches were invented by John Walker, an English chemist. This invention revolutionized daily life by providing a more convenient way to create fire compared to traditional methods like flint and steel.

Context in 1826:

Industrial Advancements: The early 19th century was marked by innovation, with new technologies emerging that would gradually improve living standards.

Ireland's Situation: In 1826, Ireland was experiencing significant challenges, including land disputes and economic hardship, particularly for tenant farmers. Despite this, the country was slowly integrating into a more modern, industrialized economy.

Global Events: Around this time, the world was witnessing the early stages of the Industrial Revolution, which would shape the decades ahead.

FOR JOHN, THE INVENTION of matches may have seemed distant, but it marked the kind of progress that would eventually influence his life, particularly if he emigrated to a place like Canada, where such innovations were eagerly adopted.

WHEN JOHN LINDSAY WAS 29 years old, the Irish Hurricane of 1836 occurred. This powerful storm hit Ireland on September 6, 1836, causing widespread destruction. It was one of the most significant weather events of the 19th century in Ireland, remembered for its violent winds and torrential rain.

Context in 1836:

Impact of the Hurricane:

Severe damage to homes, farms, and infrastructure.

Crops were destroyed, including vital potato fields, though not as catastrophic as the Great Famine a decade later.

The storm added to the hardships already faced by Ireland's rural population, especially tenant farmers.

SOCIAL CONDITIONS:

The majority of Ireland's population relied on subsistence farming.

Landlords often demanded rent despite the destruction of crops, deepening tenant struggles.

FOR JOHN LINDSAY, LIVING in Ireland at the time, the hurricane would have been a significant event. If he came from a farming family, the storm might have caused personal or economic hardships, shaping his decision to emigrate later.

WHEN JOHN LINDSAY WAS 35 years old in 1845, The Irish Famine (or Great Famine) began to take its devastating toll. The famine, which was caused by a potato blight, led to mass starvation, disease, and death in Ireland. The blight, which struck the potato crop—one of the country's main food staples—resulted in widespread crop failures.

Key events of 1845:

The Potato Blight: The disease hit Ireland's potato crops hard in 1845, leading to crop failure and food shortages. Potatoes had been the primary food source for much of the rural population, especially the poor.

Start of the Famine: By the winter of 1845-1846, Ireland faced a severe famine that would last for several years. The famine led to the deaths of approximately one million people and the emigration of over a million more.

Emigration Waves: The famine was one of the primary drivers behind the massive emigration of Irish people to countries such as Canada, the United States, and Australia. Many families, including those of John Lindsay's generation, left in search of better opportunities or to escape the grim conditions back home.

CONTEXT FOR JOHN LINDSAY:

At 35, John Lindsay would have witnessed the early days of the famine, which began affecting rural families who depended on potato crops for their survival.

If he lived in a rural area, like many Irish tenants, he may have faced hunger or loss of income due to crop failures.

The Irish Famine would have pushed many, including John, to consider emigration as a way to escape starvation and poverty, prompting many to leave Ireland in the coming years, especially as conditions worsened in 1846-1847.

BY THE END OF THE DECADE, John may have made the decision to leave Ireland for Canada, where the promise of land and a fresh start drew many immigrants.

BY 1861, JOHN LINDSAY, at the age of 51, would have experienced a period of significant change both in Ireland and Canada. Living in Storrington, Ontario, as a shoemaker and a Presbyterian, John was part of a growing immigrant community that had settled in Canada, especially after the turmoil caused by the Irish Famine.

Context of Life in 1861:

Storrington, Ontario: By 1861, the region was largely rural, with settlers engaged in farming, trade, and artisan crafts. Storrington was part of Frontenac County, a place where many Irish immigrants, like John, found new opportunities after their arrival in Canada.

Life as a Shoemaker: As a shoemaker, John would have been part of the growing artisan trades that served the local community. He likely worked with leather and other materials to create shoes, boots, and other footwear. In a small rural community like Storrington, shoemakers were important to the daily needs of families.

Presbyterian Community: As a Presbyterian, John would have been part of a relatively strong Protestant community in Ontario, particularly given the area's history of Scottish and Irish Presbyterian settlers. The Presbyterian church was an essential part of the community's social life, providing a place for worship, socializing, and community support.

THE POLITICAL LANDSCAPE of 1861:

Canada in 1861: In 1861, Canada was still a collection of British colonies. However, tensions were rising around the idea of confederation (which would happen in 1867).

Immigrant Experience: John Lindsay would have been part of a group of immigrants whose lives were shaped by the Irish Famine and the promise of a better life in Canada. Many immigrants sought stability in farming, but some, like John, pursued trades to sustain their families.

FAMILY LIFE:

Marriage and Family: At 51, John would have likely been married for several years, and his family might have included children who were growing up in this new Canadian environment. Depending on the age of his children, they may have been helping with his shoe making business or starting their own lives in Canada.

OVERALL, 1861 WOULD have been a year of relative stability for John Lindsay after the turbulence of his early life in Ireland. He was likely focused on supporting his family and contributing to his community in Storrington, a small town that offered the opportunity to live away from the hardships he had faced in Ireland.

MARGERET (BALLENTYNE) LINDSAY

MARGERET (BALLENTYNE) LINDSAY[37]

Margaret Lindsay, born in Ireland in 1820, would have lived through a period of significant historical events that shaped both her personal life and the broader context in which she lived. In 1861, when she was 41, she would have been married to John Lindsay, living in Storrington, Ontario, and raising a family.

Life in 1820s Ireland:

Political and Social Climate: Ireland in the 1820s was under British rule, and it was a period marked by significant hardship and unrest. Margaret would have witnessed the tail end of the Act of Union (1801), which united Ireland with Great Britain. The Irish population faced severe political repression, economic struggles, and religious tension between Catholics and Protestants.

Famine and Emigration: While Margaret's birth predates the Irish Famine (1845–1852), she would have been acutely aware of the difficulties it brought to Irish families. Many Irish, including those from her generation, would have left during or shortly after the famine, seeking new opportunities in places like Canada.

MARGARET IN CANADA:

Emigration to Canada: By the time she was in her 20s, Ireland was in the midst of the Irish Famine, and many families were forced to emigrate to escape the economic collapse and famine. Given that Margaret was born in Ireland in 1820 and was 25 when the Irish Immigration of 1845 took place, she may have been part of the large wave of Irish immigrants who fled to Canada during and after the famine years.

Settling in Storrington: After emigrating to Canada West (now Ontario), Margaret would have settled with her husband, John, in Storrington in 1861. By then, many Irish immigrants had established themselves in rural communities like Storrington, often working as farmers, tradesmen, or laborers.

LIFE AS A MARRIED WOMAN:

Marriage and Family Life: By 1861, Margaret was likely married to John Lindsay for over 20 years. They would have had children together and were raising them in a rural, immigrant-heavy community. As the wife of a shoemaker and a Presbyterian, she would have participated in the domestic life of the community, likely helping manage the household and, possibly, assisting John with his shoe making business.

Presbyterian Faith: As a Presbyterian, Margaret would have been an active member of the Protestant community in Storrington. Her religious practices would have likely been central to her daily life, offering a sense of stability and community in an unfamiliar land.

OVERALL CONTEXT IN 1861:

Canada in 1861: At the time, Canada was still a British colony, but the country was experiencing significant social and political change. The coming years would lead to Confederation in 1867. The Irish community, with which Margaret was closely associated, played a key role in shaping the social fabric of places like Storrington.

Settler Life: Living as a settler in a rural town in Canada West, Margaret would have faced the usual challenges of frontier life: managing a household, supporting her husband's work, and raising children. The Canadian climate, agricultural work, and family responsibilities were all part of her daily routine.

BY 1861, MARGARET HAD likely found a sense of stability in her new life in Canada, but she would have carried with her the memory of Ireland's turbulent times and the challenges of emigration. Her life would have centered on her home, her family, and her faith, all while contributing to her community in Storrington.

https://billiongraves.com/cemetery/Carlow-United-Cemetery/882534/volunteer

SAMUEL LINDSAY

SAMUEL LINDSAY[38]

Samuel Lindsay, born June 26, 1834, in Storrington, Ontario, was the son of John and Margaret Lindsay, Irish immigrants. As the child of settlers, Samuel would have grown up in a developing rural community, shaped by the challenges and opportunities of pioneer life in Upper Canada (later Canada West).

Samuel's Early Life (1830s-1840s):

Childhood on the Frontier: Born just a year before the Upper and Lower Canadian Rebellions (1837-1838), Samuel's early years were spent in a province experiencing political unrest and a push for responsible government. His family, likely preoccupied with farming or shoemaking, would have focused on building a stable life.

Daily Life: Growing up in Storrington, Samuel would have assisted his family with farming tasks or other manual labor. Education would have been limited but valued. Rural schooling emphasized basic literacy and arithmetic, though much of Samuel's learning likely came from practical experience.

HISTORICAL MILESTONES in His Youth:

1. Upper and Lower Canadian Rebellions (1837-1838): Although Samuel was too young to understand, these events would have influenced local politics and his family's view on governance.

2. PRINCIPLE OF RESPONSIBLE Government (1848): At age 14, Samuel lived during this key political shift, which granted more autonomy to local governments within Canada.

3. IRISH FAMINE IMMIGRATION (1845-1852): While his parents likely arrived in Canada earlier, Samuel would have seen the influx of Irish immigrants during his teenage years, shaping the demographic and cultural landscape of Ontario.

LIFE IN 1861:

By the time of the 1861 Census, Samuel was 27 years old, presumably Presbyterian, and living in Storrington, Ontario, likely working as a farmer or assisting with the family business. As part of a religious and industrious immigrant community, Samuel's role would have been pivotal in supporting his family and contributing to the local economy.

A Glimpse into His World:

Community: Samuel would have been part of a tight-knit rural settlement with many Irish families like his own. Neighbors often depended on each other for trade, labor, and community support.

Religion: As Presbyterians, the Lindsays were likely active in church activities, which played a central role in both spiritual life and social gatherings.

SAMUEL LINDSAY'S LIFE bridged the worlds of Irish heritage and Canadian settlement, embodying the resilience and determination of immigrant families in building a new future.

[Sydenham Cemetery, South Frontenac, Frontenac, Ontario, Canada | BillionGraves Cemetery and Images](https://billiongraves.com/cemetery/Sydenham-Cemetery/163242/volunteer)

MARTHA LINDSAY

MARTHA LINDSAY[39]

Mary Martha Lindsay, born August 28, 1838, in Kingston, Canada West, was the younger sister of Samuel Lindsay and the daughter of John and Margaret Lindsay, Irish immigrants. Her birth in Kingston—a growing urban center—places her in a community pivotal to Upper Canada's (later Canada West's) development during the mid-19th century.

Early Life in Kingston (1838-1850s):

Infancy and Childhood: Born a year after the Upper and Lower Canadian Rebellions (1837-1838), Mary Martha entered the world during a period of political and social transition. Kingston, serving as a temporary capital of the Province of Canada from 1841-1844, was a hub of trade, military, and administrative activity.

Urban vs. Rural Experience: Unlike her brother Samuel, who was born in Storrington, Mary Martha's birth in Kingston suggests that the Lindsay family spent time in a more urbanized environment, with greater access to education, commerce, and cultural influences.

HISTORICAL CONTEXT in Her Youth:

1. 1841-1844: As Kingston served briefly as the capital, Mary Martha would have lived in a city buzzing with political discussions and infrastructure development.

2. IRISH FAMINE IMMIGRATION (1845-1852): At age 7, Mary Martha witnessed the arrival of many Irish immigrants escaping the famine. This likely resonated with her family's own Irish roots.

---

3. RESPONSIBLE GOVERNMENT (1848): At age 10, she lived through this important political milestone, which began to shape the democratic identity of Canada.

LIFE IN 1861:

By 1861, Mary Martha would have been 23 years old, likely Presbyterian, and living either with her parents or nearby in Storrington, Ontario, given the family's migration to the rural township. As a young adult, she may have been involved in domestic duties, religious activities, or even assisting with her family's farming or shoemaking business.

The World of Mary Martha in 1861:

Opportunities for Women: While constrained by Victorian societal norms, women like Mary Martha were often the backbone of family life, managing households and contributing to the community. Education for women was increasingly valued, particularly in Protestant communities, though career opportunities were limited to fields like teaching or domestic service.

Community Engagement: Presbyterian women often played a key role in church activities, from organizing events to supporting missions.

MARY MARTHA LINDSAY'S life, beginning in Kingston and later moving to rural Storrington, illustrates the dynamic experiences of a family navigating the challenges and opportunities of 19th-century Canada West.

GENEALOGY ITINERARY:

Day 1: Kingston, Ontario

1.

Kingston City Hall and Archives

- Start your journey at the Kingston City Hall to explore local archives and historical records from the mid-19th century.

- Look for birth records from 1849 to confirm details about Mary Martha Lindsay's birth.

1.

St. Andrew's Presbyterian Church

- Visit this historic church to search for baptismal records and other church documents that might mention Mary or her family.

2.

Kingston Frontenac Public Library

- Check the genealogy section for local history books, newspapers, and other resources that might provide context about the Lindsay family.

Day 2: Storrington, Ontario

1.

Storrington Township Archives

- Investigate local records from the 1860s to find information about Mary Martha Lindsay's life in Storrington.

- Look for census records from 1861 to confirm her residence and family details

Presbytery Records[1]

1.

Local Presbyterian Church Records• Visit the nearest Presbyterian church to search for membership records, marriage records, and other documents related to the Lindsay family

The Presbyterian Record[2]

2.

Lennox and Addington County Museum and Archives

- Explore additional regional archives that might hold relevant documents, such as land records, wills, and other legal documents.

Day 3: Online Research and Follow-up

1.

Library and Archives Canada• Use online databases to search for birth, marriage, and death records, as well as census data

Genealogy[3]

---

1. https://presbyterianarchives.ca/finding-aids/presbytery-records/

2. https://presbyterianarchives.ca/the-presbyterian-record/

3. https://presbyterianarchives.ca/genealogy/

- Look for any digitized church records or other documents that might be available online.

1.

The Presbyterian Church in Canada Archives• Access the Presbyterian Church archives for genealogical records and historical documents

The Presbyterian Church in Canada Archives[4]

- CHECK FOR ANY MENTIONS of the Lindsay family in church publications or records.

1.

Genealogy Websites

- Utilize websites like Ancestry.ca and FamilySearch.org to search for additional records and connect with other researchers who might have information about the Lindsay family.

This itinerary should provide a comprehensive approach to tracing the life and family history of Mary Martha Lindsay. Good luck with your research!

---

4. https://presbyterianarchives.ca/

THOMAS LINDSAY

THOMAS LINDSAY[40]

Thomas Lindsay, born November 18, 1849, in Sunbury, Canada West, was the younger brother of Mary Martha and Samuel Lindsay, and the son of John and Margaret Lindsay. His birth in Sunbury, a small community within Frontenac County, marks a shift in the Lindsay family's location and lifestyle, likely toward a more rural and agrarian setting.

Historical Context Surrounding Thomas's Birth:

Canada West in 1849: This was a period of rapid change in the colony. The economic focus was shifting from fur trading to agriculture and industry, and rural communities like Sunbury were essential for supplying the growing urban centers.

Healthcare and Childbirth: In rural settings, childbirth often occurred at home, assisted by midwives or family members. The infant mortality rate was high, but Thomas's survival indicates he was born into a relatively stable household.

LIFE IN THE 1850S:

Early Childhood: Thomas grew up during a time when rural families relied heavily on children for farm labor. By the age of five or six, he may have been helping with light chores around the farm or home.

Community Life: Sunbury was a close-knit community where churches, schools, and local events were integral to daily life. As

Presbyterians, the Lindsays would have been active in their congregation, providing both social and spiritual grounding.

KEY EVENTS IN THOMAS'S Early Years:

1. 1850s Agricultural Boom: The expansion of farmland and improvements in farming techniques would have influenced the Lindsay family's livelihood in Sunbury.

2. CANADIAN EDUCATION Act (1850): As schools became more accessible, Thomas likely attended a local one-room schoolhouse, learning basic reading, writing, and arithmetic alongside his siblings.

LIFE BY 1861:

By 1861, Thomas was 11 years old, likely attending school while also contributing to the family farm. Living in Storrington Township, the Lindsays would have maintained a Presbyterian household, with religious observances playing a significant role in their daily lives.

The World of an 11-Year-Old in Rural Canada West:

Education: Children in his age group typically received a basic education, with attendance dependent on farm responsibilities and seasonal demands.

Chores and Responsibilities: Thomas would have been expected to take on age-appropriate tasks, such as feeding livestock, collecting firewood, or helping with planting and harvesting.

Social Connections: Rural communities offered limited leisure activities for children, but church gatherings, school events, and seasonal festivities provided opportunities for socializing.

THOMAS LINDSAY'S EARLY years reflect the realities of a rural upbringing in mid-19th-century Canada West, shaped by both family dynamics and the broader social and economic changes of the time.

GENEALOGY ITINERARY:

Day 1: Sunbury, Ontario

1.

Sunbury Historical Society

- Begin your journey at the local historical society to explore records and documents from the mid-19th century.

- Look for birth records from 1849 to confirm details about Thomas Lindsay's birth.

1.

Local Presbyterian Church

- Visit the nearest Presbyterian church to search for baptismal records and other church documents that might mention Thomas or his family.

2.

Frontenac County Archives

- Check the archives for local history books, newspapers, and other resources that might provide context about the Lindsay family.

Day 2: Storrington, Ontario

1.

Storrington Township Archives

• Investigate local records from the 1860s to find information about Thomas Lindsay's life in Storrington.

• Look for census records from 1861 to confirm his residence and family details

Presbytery Records[1]

1.

Local Presbyterian Church Records• Visit the nearest Presbyterian church to search for membership records, marriage records, and other documents related to the Lindsay family

The Presbyterian Record[2]

2.

Lennox and Addington County Museum and Archives

• Explore additional regional archives that might hold relevant documents, such as land records, wills, and other legal documents.

Day 3: Online Research and Follow-up

1.

---

1. https://presbyterianarchives.ca/finding-aids/presbytery-records/

2. https://presbyterianarchives.ca/the-presbyterian-record/

Library and Archives Canada• Use online databases to search for birth, marriage, and death records, as well as census data

Genealogy[3]

• LOOK FOR ANY DIGITIZED church records or other documents that might be available online.

1.

The Presbyterian Church in Canada Archives• Access the Presbyterian Church archives for genealogical records and historical documents

The Presbyterian Church in Canada Archives[4]

• CHECK FOR ANY MENTIONS of the Lindsay family in church publications or records.

1.

Genealogy Websites• Utilize websites like Ancestry.ca and FamilySearch.org to search for additional records and connect with other researchers who might have information about the Lindsay family

Search: Births, Marriages and Deaths recorded in Canada - Library and Archives Canada[5]

---

3. https://presbyterianarchives.ca/genealogy/

4. https://presbyterianarchives.ca/

5. https://www.bac-lac.gc.ca/eng/discover/vital-statistics-births-marriages-deaths/births-marriages-deaths-recorded/Pages/search.aspx

THIS ITINERARY SHOULD provide a comprehensive approach to tracing the life and family history of Thomas Lindsay. Good luck with your research!

ELIZABETH ANN LINDSAY

ELIZABETH ANN LINDSAY[41]

Elizabeth Ann Lindsay, born June 2, 1856, in Inverary, Canada West, was the youngest sibling in the Lindsay family. Her birth in Inverary, a small rural community within Frontenac County, reflects the family's continued presence in this region. As the daughter of John and Margaret Lindsay, Elizabeth would have grown up in a Presbyterian household alongside her older siblings Samuel, Mary Martha, and Thomas.

Historical Context at Elizabeth Ann's Birth:

1856 in Canada West: This was a time of steady population growth and agricultural development. Rural communities like Inverary were vital for supporting urban centers with agricultural products.

Family Life in the 1850s: Elizabeth's arrival would have brought new responsibilities to her older siblings, as large families typically shared childcare duties. Her parents, John (a shoemaker) and Margaret, would have ensured she was raised with strong moral and religious values.

LIFE IN INVERARY:

Inverary's Role: This small village served as a hub for surrounding farms, with essential services like a general store, blacksmith, and Presbyterian church. These institutions likely played a role in the Lindsay family's daily life.

Rural Upbringing: Elizabeth would have experienced a childhood defined by rural simplicity, with plenty of outdoor play and a tight-knit community atmosphere.

THE WORLD OF A YOUNG Girl in the Late 1850s:

1. Home Life: As the youngest child, Elizabeth likely spent her earliest years surrounded by the care and protection of her older siblings, particularly Mary Martha, who was nearly 18 years her senior.

2. COMMUNITY INVOLVEMENT: Church attendance would have been central to her upbringing, with Sundays reserved for worship and fellowship.

3. EDUCATION: BY THE time she reached school age, Elizabeth likely attended a local one-room schoolhouse, where she would have learned basic literacy and numeracy skills.

LIFE BY 1861:

By 1861, Elizabeth Ann was 5 years old, living in Storrington Township with her family. She would have been too young to perform significant chores but old enough to begin helping with simple tasks around the household. At this stage, her world revolved around family, church, and the rhythms of rural life.

Elizabeth Ann Lindsay's early years offer a glimpse into the life of a young girl in mid-19th-century Canada West, shaped by family, faith, and the rural environment of Inverary.

GENEALOGY ITINERARY

Day 1: Inverary, Ontario

1.

Inverary Historical Society

- Start your journey at the local historical society to explore records and documents from the mid-19th century.

- Look for birth records from 1853 to confirm details about Elizabeth Ann Lindsay's birth.

1.

Local Presbyterian Church

- Visit the nearest Presbyterian church to search for baptismal records and other church documents that might mention Elizabeth or her family.

2.

Frontenac County Archives

- Check the archives for local history books, newspapers, and other resources that might provide context about the Lindsay family.

Day 2: Storrington, Ontario

1.

Storrington Township Archives

- Investigate local records from the 1860s to find information about Elizabeth Ann Lindsay's life in Storrington.

- Look for census records from 1861 to confirm her residence and family details

National Records[1]

1.

Local Presbyterian Church Records• Visit the nearest Presbyterian church to search for membership records, marriage records, and other documents related to the Lindsay family

Genealogy[2]

2.

Lennox and Addington County Museum and Archives

- Explore additional regional archives that might hold relevant documents, such as land records, wills, and other legal documents.

Day 3: Online Research and Follow-up

1.

Library and Archives Canada• Use online databases to search for birth, marriage, and death records, as well as census data

https://www.familysearch.org/search/catalog/313462

- LOOK FOR ANY DIGITIZED church records or other documents that might be available online

---

1. https://presbyterianarchives.ca/finding-aids/national-records/
2. https://presbyterianarchives.ca/genealogy/

ECHOES OF STORRINGTON

Search: Births, Marriages and Deaths recorded in Canada - Library and Archives Canada[3]

1.

The Presbyterian Church in Canada Archives• Access the Presbyterian Church archives for genealogical records and historical documents

Genealogy[4]

• CHECK FOR ANY MENTIONS of the Lindsay family in church publications or records.

1.

Genealogy Websites• Utilize websites like Ancestry.ca and FamilySearch.org to search for additional records and connect with other researchers who might have information about the Lindsay family

---

THIS ITINERARY SHOULD provide a comprehensive approach to tracing the life and family history of Elizabeth Ann Lindsay. Good luck with your research!

---

3. https://www.bac-lac.gc.ca/eng/discover/vital-statistics-births-marriages-deaths/births-marriages-deaths-recorded/Pages/search.aspx

4. https://presbyterianarchives.ca/genealogy/

JOSEPH ALLEN LINDSAY

JOSEPH ALLEN LINDSAY[42]

Joseph Allen Lindsay, born in 1857 in Canada West, was the youngest son of John and Margaret Lindsay. Growing up in a rural, Presbyterian household in Storrington Township, Joseph Allen would have been surrounded by his older siblings and immersed in the agricultural and small-community lifestyle of the time.

Historical Context at Joseph Allen's Birth:

1857 in Canada West: This was a time of continued agricultural expansion and infrastructure development in Upper Canada (Canada West). Rural families like the Lindsays benefited from emerging transportation networks, such as improved roads and waterways, which connected small communities to larger markets.

Family Dynamics: As the youngest son, Joseph would have been doted on by his siblings, particularly Elizabeth Ann, who was just a year older.

LIFE IN THE LINDSAY Household:

Home Environment: The Lindsay household would have been bustling with activity, with older siblings assisting in household chores and farming. Joseph, as the baby of the family, likely had fewer responsibilities in his earliest years.

Community and Church: The Presbyterian faith would have been central to Joseph's upbringing, with regular church attendance and religious education shaping his moral and social development.

Education: When he reached school age, Joseph would have attended the local one-room schoolhouse, where he learned reading, writing, and arithmetic, alongside lessons in scripture and practical skills.

BY 1861:

In the 1861 Census of Canada, Joseph Allen Lindsay is 4 years old, Presbyterian, and living with his family in Storrington Township, Ontario. At this age, he would have been too young to contribute much to farm work but old enough to begin exploring the world around him and forming bonds with his siblings.

Joseph Allen's childhood, like that of his siblings, was rooted in the rhythms of rural life in mid-19th-century Canada West, shaped by family, faith, and the promise of a growing nation.

MARY JANE LINDSAY

MARY JANE LINDSAY[43]

Mary Jane Lindsay, born in 1860 in Inverary, Canada West, was the youngest daughter of John and Margaret Lindsay. As the youngest of a large family, Mary Jane would have been born into a household already bustling with activity from her older siblings, ranging in age from their 20s to toddlers.

Historical Context in 1860:

Canada West (Ontario): By this time, Canada West was becoming more settled and developed. Railways and improved infrastructure connected rural areas like Inverary to larger markets and towns.

Rural Life: Inverary was a small, close-knit community where families worked together to manage farms or small trades, like her father John's work as a shoemaker.

MARY JANE IN THE FAMILY:

A New Addition: Being the youngest, Mary Jane would have been cared for not only by her parents but also by her older siblings, particularly those still at home, such as Elizabeth Ann (4) and Joseph Allen (3).

Faith and Community: As Presbyterians, the Lindsay family likely celebrated her birth with religious significance, and Mary Jane would have been baptized in the local church.

Daily Life: Mary Jane's earliest years would have been spent in the safety of her home, surrounded by her family's strong work ethic and faith.

BY 1861:

In the 1861 Census of Canada, Mary Jane Lindsay is listed as 1 year old, Presbyterian, and living with her family in Storrington Township, Ontario. At this age, her days would have been filled with care from her mother, Margaret, and the bustling activity of life on the family property.

Mary Jane's birth added to the legacy of the Lindsay family in Inverary, tying her to the rural yet developing community of Canada West.

THOMAS YOUNG

THOMAS YOUNG[44]

Thomas Young, born in 1803 in Ireland, entered the world during a time of political and social change in the country.

Ireland in 1803:

Political Climate: This was a period of unrest. The United Irishmen's rebellion of 1798 had ended in defeat, but the desire for Irish independence persisted. In 1803, Robert Emmet led a failed uprising in Dublin, a pivotal event in Irish history.

Rural Life: Most Irish families, particularly in rural areas, were tenant farmers living under challenging conditions. Subsistence farming was common, and the majority of the population depended on the potato as a staple crop.

Economic Challenges: Landholdings were small and often heavily taxed. The Act of Union in 1801 had joined Ireland with Great Britain, but many Irish people saw little improvement in their living standards.

THOMAS'S EARLY YEARS:

Childhood: Growing up in early 19th-century Ireland, Thomas likely experienced the hardships of rural life, with limited access to education and opportunities.

WHEN THOMAS YOUNG WAS 14 years old, in 1817, the first version of the bicycle—known as the Draisine or dandy horse—was invented by Karl von Drais in Germany.

This early bicycle had no pedals and was propelled by the rider pushing their feet against the ground. It represented a significant innovation in personal transportation, though it would take decades for the bicycle to evolve into its modern form.

At the time, such advancements likely had little direct impact on Thomas's rural Irish life, but they marked the beginning of an era of mechanical invention that would shape the 19th century. By the time bicycles became widely popular in the late 19th century, Thomas was likely settled in Canada, witnessing how new technologies transformed transportation and mobility in his adopted country.

WHEN THOMAS YOUNG WAS 23 years old, in 1826, John Walker, an English chemist, invented the first practical friction match. These matches, known as "Lucifers," were struck against a rough surface to ignite.

The invention of matches revolutionized everyday life, making fire-starting far easier and safer than relying on flint, steel, or other older methods. For Thomas, who was living in Ireland at the time, this innovation might have been a fascinating development, though it would have taken some time before matches became affordable and widely available in rural areas.

WHEN THOMAS YOUNG WAS 36 years old, in 1839, the Irish Hurricane struck on August 24th. This devastating storm is considered one of the most severe to hit Ireland. It caused widespread destruction, with thousands of homes damaged, crops ruined, and numerous lives lost. The storm hit during a time when Ireland was already struggling with poverty and food insecurity, compounding the hardships faced by many families.

For Thomas, living in Ireland during this period, the hurricane likely brought significant challenges, as communities came together to rebuild and survive the aftermath. It would have been a notable event in his life, remembered for its ferocity and the difficulties it caused.

WHEN THOMAS YOUNG WAS 42 years old, in 1845, the Irish immigration wave began due to the Great Irish Famine (1845–1852). The failure of the potato crop, a staple food for many Irish families, led to widespread starvation, disease, and economic hardship. Over a million people emigrated from Ireland during this time, seeking refuge in countries like Canada, the United States, and Australia.

As someone in his early forties, Thomas may have witnessed the initial stages of the famine's impact, including food shortages, evictions, and emigration. If he emigrated around this time or later, his decision to leave Ireland may have been influenced by the harsh conditions and lack of opportunities at home. If he remained in Ireland during this period, he would have experienced the social and economic upheaval firsthand, likely making survival a daily struggle.

BY 1861, AT 58 YEARS old, Thomas Young was living in Storrington, Ontario, working as a farmer and practicing as an Anglican.

As an Irish immigrant, he would have established himself in the region, contributing to the agricultural development of the area. Storrington, part of Canada West (modern-day Ontario), was a growing community at the time. Farming was a common occupation, and Thomas likely worked hard to cultivate the land and sustain his family.

His Anglican faith suggests he was part of a local congregation, which often served as a social and spiritual hub for settlers, providing a sense of community in a new and challenging environment. By 1861, life in Storrington would have been more settled compared to his early years as an immigrant, but he still faced the hard work and unpredictability of farming in rural Canada.

GENEALOGY ITINERARY:

Day 1: Online Research for Irish Records

1.

FamilySearch and Ancestry• Start by searching for Thomas Young's birth records in Ireland using online databases like FamilySearch and Ancestry

Ireland Online Genealogy Records • FamilySearch[1]

Ireland Births and Baptisms, 1620-1881[2]

• LOOK FOR BAPTISMAL records, which might provide additional details about his family and place of birth.

1.

Irish Genealogy Websites• Utilize websites like IrishGenealogy.ie and RootsIreland.ie to search for parish records, including births, marriages, and deaths

---

[1] https://www.familysearch.org/en/wiki/Ireland_Online_Genealogy_Records

[2] https://www.familysearch.org/search/collection/1584963

Ireland Online Genealogy Records • FamilySearch[3]

DAY 2: STORRINGTON, Ontario

1.

Storrington Township Archives

• Investigate local records from the 1860s to find information about Thomas Young's life in Storrington.

• Look for census records from 1861 to confirm his residence and family details

Archives | Resources | Anglican Diocese of Ontario[4]

1.

Local Anglican Church Records• Visit the nearest Anglican church to search for membership records, marriage records, and other documents related to Thomas Young

Archives | Resources | Anglican Diocese of Ontario[5]

• The Anglican Diocese of Ontario Archives in Kingston might have relevant records, including baptisms, marriages, and burials

Archives | Resources | Anglican Diocese of Ontario[6]

1.

---

3. https://www.familysearch.org/en/wiki/Ireland_Online_Genealogy_Records

4. https://ontario.anglican.ca/resources/archives

5. https://ontario.anglican.ca/resources/archives

6. https://ontario.anglican.ca/resources/archives

Lennox and Addington County Museum and Archives

- Explore additional regional archives that might hold relevant documents, such as land records, wills, and other legal documents.

Day 3: Kingston, Ontario

1.

Kingston Frontenac Public Library

- Check the genealogy section for local history books, newspapers, and other resources that might provide context about Thomas Young and his family.

2.

Anglican Diocese of Ontario Archives• Access the archives for genealogical records and historical documents related to the Anglican Church in the region

Archives | Resources | Anglican Diocese of Ontario[7]

- LOOK FOR ANY MENTIONS of the Young family in church publications or records.

Day 4: Online Research and Follow-up

1.

Library and Archives Canada• Use online databases to search for birth, marriage, and death records, as well as census data

Parish and related birth, marriage and death records[8]

---

7. https://ontario.anglican.ca/resources/archives

- LOOK FOR ANY DIGITIZED church records or other documents that might be available online.

1.

Genealogy Websites• Utilize websites like Ancestry.ca and FamilySearch.org to search for additional records and connect with other researchers who might have information about the Young family

https://www.familysearch.org/en/wiki/Ontario_Church_Records

THIS ITINERARY SHOULD provide a comprehensive approach to tracing the life and family history of Thomas Young. Good luck with your research!

---

8. https://library-archives.canada.ca/eng/collection/research-help/genealogy-family-history/birth-marriage-death-records/pages/parish-records.aspx

MARTHA (UNKNOWN) YOUNG

MARTHA (UNKNOWN) YOUNG[45]

In 1821, Ireland was under British rule, experiencing a turbulent period marked by economic hardship, political unrest, and social inequality. Life in Ireland at that time was heavily shaped by agrarian culture, with most of the population working as tenant farmers on land owned by wealthy landlords. Ireland's economy was largely agrarian, and the majority of the population depended on farming for their livelihoods, particularly the cultivation of crops like potatoes, which were a staple food.

However, the early 19th century in Ireland was also a time of great distress. The country was dealing with the aftereffects of the Napoleonic Wars (which had strained the economy) and a system of land ownership that was inequitable, with many tenant farmers living in poverty. The Irish were subjected to heavy taxes and rent, and many faced dire living conditions, particularly in rural areas.

The Irish Rebellion of 1798, though earlier in the century, had left a legacy of tension between Irish Catholics (who made up the majority of the population) and the Protestant ruling class, particularly in terms of politics and land ownership. Though the rebellion had been suppressed, it contributed to a rising sense of Irish nationalism that would continue to develop in the 19th century.

The 1820s were also a period of political change, though Ireland did not yet have full representation in the British Parliament, and the majority of the population had little political power. In 1829, the Catholic Emancipation Act was passed, which allowed Catholics to hold public office and gave them more political rights. This was a significant shift, as Irish Catholics had been historically excluded from many civil rights, and it reflected the growing influence of Irish nationalist movements.

The Great Famine would not strike for another two decades, but even in 1821, many Irish families lived in precarious conditions, with limited access to food and medical care. Many rural Irish families lived in small, thatched cottages with basic furnishings. Education was limited, and life expectancy was relatively low, particularly in rural areas.

Overall, life in Ireland in 1821 was challenging for most people, particularly for the rural poor. Martha Young, born into this environment, would have experienced a life shaped by hardship, with limited access to resources and opportunities. It was likely a time when many sought a better life elsewhere, with emigration to countries like Canada becoming a more common option for those seeking to escape poverty and hardship.

MARTHA YOUNG, BORN in 1821, would have been 5 years old in 1826, the year the first reliable friction match was invented by John Walker in England. This invention was a significant milestone in the development of everyday life, as it allowed people to easily light fires, replacing earlier methods like flint and tinder. Matches quickly became an essential household item, contributing to greater convenience in daily living, especially in rural areas like those Martha would have known in Ireland.

However, even though the match was invented during her early childhood, it would take some time before they were widely available, and their use became common among the general public. For a young child like Martha, life in 1826 would still have been more reliant on older methods for lighting fires, such as flint and steel, or the use of candles, which would later be made easier with the invention of matches.

IN 1839, WHEN MARTHA Young was 18 years old, the Irish Hurricane occurred. This violent storm, which devastated parts of Ireland, was one of the most extreme weather events of the 19th century for the country. The hurricane hit particularly hard in the south and west, causing extensive damage to buildings, crops, and trees. It was described as a "tempest of the greatest violence" that lasted several days, bringing floods, destruction, and loss of life.

For Martha, living through this event would have been a traumatic experience, especially if she lived in one of the affected regions. Ireland in the early 19th century was still largely rural, with many people relying on farming for their livelihood. The destruction of crops and infrastructure would have had significant economic impacts, leading to hardship for many families.

The hurricane also contributed to the sense of vulnerability that many in Ireland felt during this period, as they were already dealing with political instability, social unrest, and economic struggles. For Martha, the event likely marked a pivotal moment in her young adult life, one that would shape her perspective on the unpredictability of nature and life itself.

IN 1845, WHEN MARTHA Young was 24 years old, Ireland was plunged into one of the most devastating events in its history: the Great Irish Famine. The famine, caused by a potato blight that ruined crops, led to widespread starvation, disease, and death. The blight was particularly disastrous for the Irish peasantry, who relied heavily on the potato as a staple food. With the failure of the potato crop, millions of people faced hunger, and the British government's inadequate response only deepened the crisis.

During this time, Martha, like many others, might have seen the massive migration of Irish citizens to North America, especially Canada, in an attempt to escape the dire conditions. Between 1845 and 1852, about one million people left Ireland, many heading to Canada, where the British colonial authorities promised land grants to settlers.

For Martha, the famine could have led to personal hardship, and it is possible that she was part of the wave of emigrants, whether due to economic reasons, the pursuit of a better life, or to escape the famine. However, given that she was 24, she might have also witnessed the suffering around her, as communities were torn apart by the crisis. The famine and the subsequent migration would have been defining events in her life, reshaping Ireland's demographic and social landscape and impacting her decision to emigrate, if she chose to do so.

BY 1861, MARTHA YOUNG would have been 40 years old and living in Storrington, Ontario. This was a time when the Irish immigration to Canada had been significant, especially following the Great Famine of the 1840s, which caused many Irish to seek refuge and a better life in places like Ontario. Many Irish immigrants, like Martha, settled in rural areas, becoming farmers or workers in growing communities.

In Storrington, which was part of Canada West (modern-day Ontario), life for Martha would likely have involved managing a household and farm, likely alongside her husband. Since she was Anglican, she would have been part of a Christian community, and church attendance and involvement in religious activities would have been an important part of her social life.

The 1860s were a time of significant social and economic change. Canada was on the brink of Confederation (which would occur in 1867), and the country was moving toward greater political and economic development. Storrington, like many rural areas, would have been largely agricultural, with settlers establishing farms, raising livestock, and growing crops. Given the hardships Martha likely faced as an immigrant, her life in Storrington might have offered more stability and opportunity than what she left behind in Ireland. The local Anglican church would have played a role in providing community and spiritual support in this growing frontier settlement.

By 1861, the legacy of the Irish Famine and immigration would still have been fresh in the minds of many Irish immigrants, and the transition to a new life in Canada would have been something that shaped her perspective and her family's future.

JOHN YOUNG

JOHN YOUNG[46]

John Young, born in Canada West in 1842, was the son of Thomas and Martha Young. Growing up in this period, he would have witnessed the changing landscape of Canada as it was transitioning from a British colony to the larger political entity that would eventually become Canada.

Born into a farming family, John would have been part of the growing agricultural community in Canada West (now Ontario). The 1840s were a time of expansion for settlers, as the region's population was rapidly increasing, especially with the influx of Irish immigrants following the Great Famine. His parents, both from Ireland, would have been part of this wave of immigration, seeking better opportunities in the relatively new country of Canada.

In 1861, when John was around 19 years old, he would likely have been working on the family farm with his parents. By this time, the family would have been settled into the rhythms of rural life, with farming, livestock management, and local trade taking up much of their time. John may also have been involved in the community, with ties to the local Anglican church, as his family was Anglican, which would have provided both religious and social support.

As the 1860s progressed, John would have been part of a generation that experienced significant social and political shifts, especially as the discussions around Confederation (which culminated in 1867) grew. The impact of these national developments would have had a profound effect on his life, as the country transitioned from a British colony to a confederated nation.

In short, John Young's early life in Canada West would have been shaped by his family's immigrant roots, the agricultural life of the time, and the larger political changes taking place in the young country.

WHEN JOHN YOUNG WAS 6 years old in 1848, the Principle of Responsible Government was established in Canada. This was a significant development in the political evolution of the colonies, especially in Canada West (later Ontario), where John would have lived.

The Principle of Responsible Government meant that the executive branch of the government (the Governor and his appointed officials) would be accountable to the elected legislative assembly, rather than the British Crown. It marked a shift towards self-governance for the colonies, particularly in Canada East (now Quebec) and Canada West (now Ontario).

In practical terms, this meant that the Governor could no longer override the decisions made by the elected representatives. The first major success of this principle came in 1849, with the passage of the Rebellion's Losses Bill, which was seen as an early example of responsible government in action.

For John Young and his family, this political change may not have been immediately apparent in their daily farming life, but it would have been a significant step in shaping the future of Canada. As he grew older, John would have witnessed the gradual shift toward greater autonomy for the colony, culminating in the confederation of Canada in 1867.

IN 1861, AT 19 YEARS old, John Young would have been coming into adulthood during a time of significant political and social change in Canada West (Ontario). He was likely living in a rural community, working on the farm alongside his family, and participating in the agricultural life that was typical of the region at the time.

Being Anglican, John would have been part of the Church of England, which was a prominent religious group in the area. Religion would have played a significant role in the daily life of the community, with church attendance being an important aspect of social and cultural life. Many Anglican families would have also been involved in charitable work and social gatherings through the church.

Given that it was the year of the Canadian Confederation discussions, John would have been witnessing the early signs of political unity and discussions about the future of the Canadian colonies. The 1861 Census in Canada West would have shown a population that was mostly rural and agrarian, much like John's life in Storrington. The community would have been predominantly Anglo-Canadian, and John's parents, like many others, likely had a vested interest in local politics, religion, and the changing role of Ontario in the broader Canadian context.

In short, 1861 marked a transitional period, and John would have been part of a growing generation of young people poised to help shape the future of Canada. His life, while largely centered around farming, was being influenced by the social, political, and cultural shifts of the time.

WILLIAM YOUNG

WILLIAM YOUNG[47]

In 1844, William Young would have been born during a period of growth and transition in Canada West (Ontario). The region was still largely rural and agrarian, with many families like the Youngs involved in farming. William's birth took place just one year before the Irish Immigration of 1845, when many Irish immigrants began arriving in Canada due to the Great Irish Famine.

By the time he was growing up, Canada West was experiencing significant changes, including the shift toward Responsible Government (which began in the 1840s) and the growing influence of Canadian nationalism. As an Anglican family, the Youngs would have been part of a tightly-knit religious community that played a central role in daily life.

By the time of the 1861 census, William would have been 17 years old and likely involved in the agricultural work that was a cornerstone of life in the region. If he had older siblings, he may have helped his parents, Thomas and Martha, with farming, contributing to the sustenance and development of their community in Storrington, Ontario.

Like his brother John, William would have been raised in the context of an emerging Canadian identity, witnessing the political developments that would lead to Confederation in 1867. William's formative years were marked by both local events and the broader political shifts taking place in the Canadian colonies, preparing him for the changes and opportunities that were beginning to unfold across the nation.

RICHARD YOUNG

RICHARD YOUNG[48]

Richard Young, born in Canada West (modern-day Ontario) in 1847, came into the world during a time of economic and political transformation in the region. Canada West was growing as a destination for immigrants, especially those fleeing hardships in Europe, such as the Irish fleeing the Great Famine, which peaked from 1845 to 1852.

As a younger son of Thomas and Martha Young, Richard would have been raised in a primarily agricultural environment. Farming families like the Youngs relied heavily on teamwork, and by the time Richard was old enough, he would have contributed to farm chores alongside his siblings. The Anglican Church would have played a central role in his upbringing, shaping his moral and social life.

Richard's early childhood coincided with significant developments in Canada, such as the establishment of the Principle of Responsible Government in 1848. This set the stage for the gradual movement toward Canadian Confederation in 1867, which he would witness as a young adult.

By 1861, Richard was 14 years old, Anglican, and living in Storrington, Ontario, alongside his parents and siblings. His teenage years would have been marked by both family responsibilities on the farm and the societal changes shaping Canada West's future as part of the growing nation.

FRANCIS BLESSON

FRANCIS BLESSON[49]

Francis Blesson, born in Ireland in 1811, grew up during a tumultuous time in Irish history. His early years were shaped by the ongoing repercussions of British rule, agricultural dependency, and the growing unrest that would lead to major reforms and upheavals later in the century.

Life in Ireland in 1811

Ireland in 1811 was under British governance, with much of the population living in rural areas and relying on subsistence farming. The majority of Irish people were tenant farmers, often working small plots of land owned by absentee landlords. Poverty was widespread, especially among Catholic families, as legal and social inequalities restricted their access to land ownership, education, and political participation under the Penal Laws (though these were gradually being repealed during this period).

Agriculture dominated the economy, with potatoes being the staple crop for much of the population. While the potato provided a reliable source of nutrition, over-reliance on this single crop left many vulnerable to food shortages, a precursor to future calamities like the Great Famine.

Global Context

1811 was also a year of broader global change. The Napoleonic Wars were at their height, and their economic impact reached Ireland, leading to disruptions in trade and occasional food shortages. Social tensions were high, with secret societies such as the Ribbonmen forming to resist landlord oppression.

As Francis grew, he would witness significant events that shaped Irish history, including the Catholic Emancipation movement, the repeal of the remaining Penal Laws, and eventually the Great Famine, which drove many Irish families, including possibly his own, to emigrate.

By the time he was an adult, Francis would have been well-acquainted with the challenges of life in Ireland, from political instability to the daily struggle for survival in a land where wealth and power were concentrated in the hands of a few. If he emigrated to Canada or elsewhere, like many others, it would likely have been in pursuit of better opportunities and freedom from the hardships of rural Irish life.

WHEN FRANCIS BLESSON was 15 years old in 1826, the invention of friction matches marked a significant advancement in everyday convenience. This innovation, created by English chemist John Walker, allowed people to easily and safely ignite fires without relying on more cumbersome methods like flint and steel.

Context in Francis's Life

At this time, Francis was a teenager in Ireland, where life was still largely rural and dependent on manual labor. The availability of matches, though not immediately widespread or affordable for everyone, eventually revolutionized domestic life by making tasks like lighting fires for cooking or warmth much easier. For Francis and others in Ireland, this invention might have seemed like a small yet impressive marvel of modern ingenuity.

WHEN FRANCIS BLESSON was 28 years old, in 1839, the devastating Irish Hurricane struck on January 6th. Known as "The Night of the Big Wind" (Oíche na Gaoithe Móire in Irish), it was the most severe storm ever recorded in Ireland's history. The hurricane caused widespread destruction, with winds demolishing homes, uprooting trees, and damaging infrastructure across the island.

Context in Francis's Life

As a young adult in Ireland during this catastrophic event, Francis would have witnessed the widespread panic and devastation. Many Irish people, already struggling with poverty and inadequate housing, were severely impacted. The storm left tens of thousands homeless and resulted in numerous fatalities. It would have been a moment of fear and resilience for Francis and his community, as they worked to rebuild in the aftermath.

WHEN FRANCIS BLESSON was 34 years old, in 1845, the beginning of the Great Irish Famine (An Gorta Mór) triggered a mass wave of Irish immigration. That year marked the failure of the potato crop due to potato blight (Phytophthora infestans), a disaster for Ireland's predominantly agrarian society, where potatoes were a staple food for much of the population.

Irish Immigration Context

As the famine worsened, thousands of Irish people fled the country in search of a better life, primarily to North America, Australia, and Britain. These migrants often traveled in perilous conditions aboard "coffin ships", so named because of the high mortality rates due to disease and malnutrition during the journey.

Francis's Perspective

At 34, Francis might have been deeply affected by the exodus of friends, neighbors, and possibly family members. The societal collapse caused by starvation, eviction, and emigration would have created an atmosphere of despair. If Francis later moved to Canada, this period could have been a decisive factor in his own migration. For those who remained in Ireland, life became increasingly harsh, with over a million deaths and an additional million leaving the island during the famine years (1845–1852).

IN 1861, AT 50 YEARS old, Francis Blesson was living as a widower, Catholic, and a farmer in Storrington, Ontario. As a Catholic in Storrington, he would have been part of a minority religious group within a largely Protestant community, reflecting the broader demographic trends of the time in Ontario.

Life in Storrington for Francis Blesson:

Widower: Losing his spouse would have been a significant personal challenge. Widowers often relied heavily on extended family, neighbors, or hired help for support in both raising children (if any) and managing the farm.

Farming Life: Farming in 1861 required physical labor and resilience. Farmers like Francis would cultivate crops such as wheat, barley, oats, and potatoes while raising livestock. He would have also participated in local markets and relied on rural networks for goods and services.

Catholic Faith: As a Catholic in Ontario, Francis likely attended mass at the nearest parish church and participated in events to maintain his spiritual and cultural heritage, particularly as a first-generation immigrant from Ireland. The church also served as a support system for widowers and families during times of hardship.

Community Role: By 1861, Francis had likely been in Canada for several years, possibly moving there due to the Irish Famine or earlier economic hardships. His presence would have contributed to the growing Irish immigrant community in Ontario, bringing Irish traditions and culture to the rural landscape.

FRANCIS'S LIFE IN STORRINGTON would have been shaped by the hard realities of pioneer farming, the isolation of widowhood, and the efforts to maintain his Irish Catholic identity in a new land.

GENEALOGY ITINERARY:

Day 1: Online Research for Irish Records

1.

Irish Genealogy Websites• Start by searching for Frances Blesson's birth records in Ireland using websites like IrishGenealogy.ie and RootsIreland.ie

Irish Genealogy[1]

• LOOK FOR BAPTISMAL records, which might provide additional details about his family and place of birth.

1.

FamilySearch and Ancestry• Utilize these platforms to search for any additional records from Ireland, including parish records and civil registrations

Ireland Civil Registration, 1845-1913[2]

---

1. https://irishgenealogy.ie/en/

DAY 2: STORRINGTON, Ontario

1.

Storrington Township Archives

• Investigate local records from the 1860s to find information about Frances Blesson's life in Storrington.

• Look for census records from 1861 to confirm his residence and family details

Canada, Ontario Roman Catholic Church Records, 1760-1923[3]

1.

Local Catholic Church Records• Visit the nearest Catholic church to search for membership records, marriage records, and other documents related to Frances Blesson

Canada, Ontario Roman Catholic Church Records, 1760-1923[4]

• THE ROMAN CATHOLIC Diocese of Kingston Archives might have relevant records, including baptisms, marriages, and burials

Canada, Ontario Roman Catholic Church Records, 1760-1923[5]

---

2. https://www.familysearch.org/search/collection/2659409

3. https://www.familysearch.org/search/collection/1927566

4. https://www.familysearch.org/search/collection/1927566

5. https://www.familysearch.org/search/collection/1927566

1.

Lennox and Addington County Museum and Archives

- Explore additional regional archives that might hold relevant documents, such as land records, wills, and other legal documents.

Day 3: Kingston, Ontario

1.

Kingston Frontenac Public Library

- Check the genealogy section for local history books, newspapers, and other resources that might provide context about Frances Blesson and his family.

2.

Roman Catholic Diocese of Kingston Archives• Access the archives for genealogical records and historical documents related to the Catholic Church in the region

Canada, Ontario Roman Catholic Church Records, 1760-1923[6]

- LOOK FOR ANY MENTIONS of the Blesson family in church publications or records.

Day 4: Online Research and Follow-up

1.

Library and Archives Canada• Use online databases to search for birth, marriage, and death records, as well as census data

---

[6] https://www.familysearch.org/search/collection/1927566

Ontario, Canada Online Genealogy Records at FamilySearch - OnGenealogy[7]

• LOOK FOR ANY DIGITIZED church records or other documents that might be available online

Parish and related birth, marriage and death records[8]

1.

Genealogy Websites• Utilize websites like Ancestry.ca and FamilySearch.org to search for additional records and connect with other researchers who might have information about the Blesson family

Parish and related birth, marriage and death records[9]

THIS ITINERARY SHOULD provide a comprehensive approach to tracing the life and family history of Frances Blesson. Good luck with your research!

---

7. https://www.ongenealogy.com/listings/ontario-canada-online-genealogy-records-at-familysearch/

8. https://library-archives.canada.ca/eng/collection/research-help/genealogy-family-history/birth-marriage-death-records/pages/parish-records.aspx

9. https://library-archives.canada.ca/eng/collection/research-help/genealogy-family-history/birth-marriage-death-records/pages/parish-records.aspx

[1] https://www.wikitree.com/wiki/Smith-356233#Ancestors

[2] https://www.wikitree.com/wiki/Smith-356236#Ancestors

[3] https://www.wikitree.com/wiki/Smith-356237#Ancestors

[4] https://www.wikitree.com/wiki/Smith-356240#Ancestors

[5] https://www.wikitree.com/wiki/Smith-356245#Ancestors

[6] https://www.wikitree.com/wiki/Smith-356280#Ancestors

[7] https://www.wikitree.com/wiki/Unknown-703564#Ancestors

[8] https://www.wikitree.com/wiki/Smith-356299#Ancestors

[9] https://www.wikitree.com/wiki/Unknown-703583#Ancestors

[10] https://www.wikitree.com/wiki/Smith-356301#Ancestors

[11] https://www.wikitree.com/wiki/Smith-356319#Ancestors

[12] https://www.wikitree.com/wiki/Smith-356322#Ancestors

[13] https://www.wikitree.com/wiki/Smith-356324#Ancestors

[14] https://www.wikitree.com/wiki/Smith-356328#Ancestors

[15] https://www.wikitree.com/wiki/Shaw-33148#Ancestors

[16] https://www.wikitree.com/wiki/Stewart-63393#Ancestors

[17] https://www.wikitree.com/wiki/Unknown-703628#Ancestors

[18] https://www.wikitree.com/wiki/Stewart-63399#Ancestors

[19] https://www.wikitree.com/wiki/Stewart-63400#Ancestors

[20] https://www.wikitree.com/wiki/McWatters-156#Ancestors

[21] https://www.wikitree.com/wiki/Unknown-703659#Ancestors

[22] https://www.wikitree.com/wiki/McWatters-157#Ancestors

[23] https://www.wikitree.com/wiki/McWatters-158#Ancestors

[24] https://www.wikitree.com/wiki/McWatters-159#Ancestors

[25] https://www.wikitree.com/wiki/McWatters-160#Ancestors

[26] https://www.wikitree.com/wiki/McWatters-161#Ancestors

[27] https://www.wikitree.com/wiki/Unknown-703776

[28] https://www.wikitree.com/wiki/Johnston-32170#Ancestors

[29] https://www.wikitree.com/wiki/Unknown-703676#Ancestors

[30] https://www.wikitree.com/wiki/Johnston-32172#Ancestors

[31] https://www.wikitree.com/wiki/Johnston-32176#Ancestors

[32] https://www.wikitree.com/wiki/Johnston-32178#Ancestors

[33] https://www.wikitree.com/wiki/Johnston-32181#Ancestors

[34] https://www.wikitree.com/wiki/Johnston-32184#Ancestors

[35] https://www.wikitree.com/wiki/Johnston-32185#Ancestors

[36] https://www.wikitree.com/wiki/Lindsay-9468#Ancestors

[37] https://www.wikitree.com/wiki/Unknown-703782#Ancestors

[38] https://www.wikitree.com/wiki/Lindsay-9470#Ancestors

[39] https://www.wikitree.com/wiki/Lindsay-9471#Ancestors

[40] https://www.wikitree.com/wiki/Lindsay-9472#Ancestors

[41] https://www.wikitree.com/wiki/Lindsay-9473#Ancestors

[42] https://www.wikitree.com/wiki/Lindsay-9474#Ancestors

[43] https://www.wikitree.com/wiki/Lindsay-9479#Ancestors[10]

[44] https://www.wikitree.com/wiki/Young-68649#Ancestors

[45] https://www.wikitree.com/wiki/Unknown-703872#Ancestors

[46] https://www.wikitree.com/wiki/Young-68650#Ancestors

[47] https://www.wikitree.com/wiki/Young-68651#Ancestors

[48] https://www.wikitree.com/wiki/Young-68653#Ancestors

[49] https://www.wikitree.com/wiki/Blesson-1#Ancestors

---

10. https://www.wikitree.com/wiki/Lindsay-9479#Ancestors

Don't miss out!

Visit the website below and you can sign up to receive emails whenever Angeline Gallant publishes a new book. There's no charge and no obligation.

https://books2read.com/r/B-A-QGSI-RUTJF

BOOKS 2 READ

Connecting independent readers to independent writers.

Also by Angeline Gallant

A Dragon's Diary
Dreaming of Dragons

Blood and Spirit Saga
The Rising Wind
Fate's Promise

Calling Her Heart
Whisper of the Heart
Calling Her Heart Volumes 1 & 2: A Small Town Romance Collection
No Turning Back
Calling Her Heart volumes 3 & 4
Forsake Me Not
Hear My Cry

FORGET ME NOT
Victoria, Ontario's Babies 1894 - 1895

Guardian of the Heart
Fallen Petals

Keeper Of Secrets
A Lady's Secret

Kingston's Love Chronicles
Springtime Promises

Midnight's Awakening
Heart of the Storm
Walking Through The Storm
Walking Through The Storm
Fighting the Storm
Call Me Cursed
Heart of the Storm

Secrets of the Underworld
Deklan's Dragons

Tell My Story Collection
Tell My Story: Germany 1851
Tell My Story: England 1852

Whispers From The Garrison Church

The Dervock Legacy
Echoes of Dervock

The Grave Whisperer
German Prisoners of War in Canada
Cataraqui United Church Cemetery
Whispers of Kingston
Wedding Bells in Kingston, Ontario, Canada 1923
St. Paul's Anglican Churchyard A-B
St. Paul's Anglican Churchyard C-D
St. Paul's Anglican Churchyard E - F
St. Paul's Anglican Churchyard G - H
St. Paul's Anglican Churchyard J - N
St. Paul's Anglican Churchyard O - R
St. Paul's Anglican Churchyard S - T
St. Paul's Anglican Churchyard, Kingston, Ontario T - Z
Small Graveyards & Burial Grounds: Kingston, Ontario, Canada
Cataraqui United Church Cemetery 1
Cataraqui United Church Cemetery 2
Cataraqui United Church Cemetary 3
Cataraqui United Church Cemetery 4
Cataraqui United Church Cemetery 5
Beth Israel Cemetery
Cataraqui United Church Cemetery 6
Beneath the Surface: Echoes from Beth Israel Cemetery
Grave Tales: Discovering the Lives of Beth Israel
Whispers Beneath St. Paul's
Unveiled

The Timeless Veil
Eternal Devotion

The Wolf Whisperer Series
Captured Heart
Fate's Legacy
Mohawk Valley
Cry of a Warrior
Wolf Whisperer volumes 1 & 2
Endless White
The Wolf Whisperer volumes 1 & 2

Timeless
The Time Keeper's Sanctuary

Timeless Echoes
Echoes of Storrington

Timeless Whispers of Dervock Saga
Secrets of Dervock

Standalone
Winds of Change vol 1-3

Watch for more at https://www.goodreads.com/author/show/19703964.Angeline_Gallant.

About the Author

Angeline Gallant traces her roots through generations of Old Stock Canadian heritage, her passion for genealogy as deep and enduring as the forests and fields her ancestors once walked. With a reverence for history and an eye for detail, she weaves stories from the fragments of lives left behind in letters, records, and weathered headstones.

An avid reader and devoted writer, Angeline brings the past to life with a curiosity for heraldry and a deep love for the landscapes that shaped her family's story. Each name and date she uncovers feels less like history and more like coming home, a familiar echo in the vast tapestry of time. For her, these stories are not forgotten—they live, breathing in the quiet spaces of memory and tradition, a testament to lives once lived, now eternal in the pages of her books.

Read more at https://www.goodreads.com/author/show/19703964.Angeline_Gallant.

About the Publisher

At Crest & Quill Press, we bring history to life, one story at a time. Specializing in genealogy, heraldry, and historical fiction and nonfiction, we are passionate about uncovering the past and celebrating the stories that shape our world today.

From tales of noble lineages and family legacies to immersive historical sagas, our books are crafted for readers who crave a deeper connection to their roots and a richer understanding of history. Whether you're exploring the crests of your ancestors or diving into vivid narratives of bygone eras, Crest & Quill delivers stories that resonate and endure.

With a dedication to authenticity, storytelling, and the preservation of history, Crest & Quill Press is your gateway to the past—and a celebration of its impact on the present and future.

www.ingramcontent.com/pod-product-compliance
Ingram Content Group UK Ltd.
Pitfield, Milton Keynes, MK11 3LW, UK
UKHW041843141224
452457UK00012B/612